T0008671

PLAYING CARD DIVINATION

About the Author

Stephen Ball is the author of *Elemental Divination: A Dice Oracle* and has taught and created systems of divination for over twenty years. He previously published *The Apple Branch: An English Shamanism* as Stephen Blake, and has contributed to Avalonia's anthology *Horns of Power* and to Steve Drury's *Dice Mysteries*. He lives in London, UK.

EVERY CARD TELLS A STORY

PLAYING
CARD
DIVINATION

STEPHEN BALL

LLEWELLYN PUBLICATIONS
WOODBURY, MINNESOTA

Playing Card Divination: Every Card Tells a Story © 2020 by Stephen Ball. All rights reserved. No part of this book may be used or reproduced in any manner whatsoever, including internet usage, without written permission from Llewellyn Publications, except in the case of brief quotations embodied in critical articles and reviews.

FIRST EDITION
Third Printing, 2023

Book design by Samantha Penn
Cover design by Kevin R. Brown
Editing by Laura Kurtz
Photograph on page 8 by Sunish Chabba

Llewellyn Publications is a registered trademark of Llewellyn Worldwide Ltd.

Library of Congress Cataloging-in-Publication Data
Names: Ball, Stephen, author.
Title: Playing card divination : every card tells a story / Stephen Ball.
Description: First edition. | Woodbury, Minnesota : Llewellyn Publications,
    2020. | Includes bibliographical references and index. | Summary: "Turn
    a standard deck of playing cards into a colorful divinatory system
    filled with inspiration, adventure, advice and insight"-- Provided by
    publisher.
Identifiers: LCCN 2020008059 (print) | LCCN 2020008060 (ebook) | ISBN
    9780738764900 (paperback) | ISBN 9780738765068 (ebook)
Subjects: LCSH: Divination cards. | Fortune-telling by cards.
Classification: LCC BF1778.5 .B35 2020 (print) | LCC BF1778.5 (ebook) |
    DDC 133.3/242--dc23
LC record available at https://lccn.loc.gov/2020008059
LC ebook record available at https://lccn.loc.gov/2020008060

Llewellyn Worldwide Ltd. does not participate in, endorse, or have any authority or responsibility concerning private business transactions between our authors and the public.

All mail addressed to the author is forwarded but the publisher cannot, unless specifically instructed by the author, give out an address or phone number.

Any internet references contained in this work are current at publication time, but the publisher cannot guarantee that a specific location will continue to be maintained. Please refer to the publisher's website for links to authors' websites and other sources.

Llewellyn Publications
A Division of Llewellyn Worldwide Ltd.
2143 Wooddale Drive
Woodbury, MN 55125-2989
www.llewellyn.com

Printed in the United States of America

Other Books by Stephen Ball

Elemental Divination: A Dice Oracle (Llewellyn, 2018)

To my loves. I managed to be lucky at cards
and at life, which is good fortune indeed.

ACKNOWLEDGMENTS

Many thanks to Elysia and Emily, to my proof-readers, and to the many friends who have enthusiastically helped these new systems grow.

CONTENTS

SECTION TWO
THE CARDS AND THEIR MEANINGS

SECTION THREE
EPILOGUE

SECTION FOUR
BIBLIOGRAPHY AND INDEXES

SECTION ONE
INTRODUCTION

CHAPTER ONE

HISTORY AND NEW IDEAS

Playing cards have been loved by people all over the world for centuries and have been used in divination for most of that time. Cards for playing games were known in Europe by 1375, and the first English packs were made around 1450. They are usually associated today with the glamor and risk of Poker or a spy playing in a luxurious casino, but there is also a long tradition where exactly the same playing cards were used to tell the future.

I love creating new divination systems. I've done it a lot over the years, and you can discover a rich source of new ideas from almost anything: string, coloured beads, cities, autumn leaves. The two objects I think are the easiest and cheapest to buy today—but which also have very important histories in divination—are playing cards and dice.

I previously wrote a book which introduced readers to the ancient use of dice for foretelling the future (*Elemental Divination: A Dice Oracle*, Llewellyn 2018). The other I felt I had to write was this one, because the playing card deck is a unique experience that continues to fascinate and entertain us in a way few others have over the centuries. It's a survivor, an unbroken connection to both the past and the ways in which people play with chance and luck.

The following pages will give you a complete system of divination using only a standard playing card deck. You will discover personalities within the cards: Mythic Roles such as the Hunter, the Trickster, and the Healer, and learn how they form a path of wisdom for us to follow.

A Modern Deck

Some of the traditional meanings of playing cards in divination are not very useful for today's readers. They are usually focused on three things: marriage, illness, and tall dark strangers. Back when the systems were developed, those were the most important topics!

Unfortunately, they're just not satisfying to us now. For example, a book of "Kentucky Superstitions" in the 1920s lists the court cards as "A blond man, A rather dark-haired man, an extremely dark-haired man …" and so on, leaving a quarter of the deck as only that. Other lists obsess over whether you will be successful in business, or they give different definitions of each card depending on whether the client is a man or a woman, often in a sexist way that simply doesn't apply to our lives anymore.

This new modern system was created to give readers a full set of answers and hidden wisdom without needing to ignore half of the results from historical lists. The popularity of tarot, Lenormand, and other decks today means that we are used to seeing a much wider set of ideas and themes. It's time that playing cards delivered the same deep experience.

There is no fixed set of playing card meanings for divination. Some have been written down over the years but either use a smaller number of cards or have the disappointing meanings mentioned above. More importantly, there is no history of everyone using those few fixed ideas anyway. Playing cards have always been invented and reinvented. For example, two hundred years ago the King of Clubs represented an evil man—until Mlle. Lenormand, one of the most famous card readers whose name was later applied to an entire deck, thought that the King of Clubs was a generous and helpful man instead. Many authors today use their own style which was developed from something they were taught (by someone who also changed what they were originally taught). There is not, and never has been, one "true" set of definitions for playing cards.

This flexibility is an exciting opportunity for card readers to create, to improve and to share. The more techniques and stories we give to each other, the more wisdom we will all find in this brilliant deck.

Gambit, Folly, and the Roles Within the Cards

Playing card divination usually gives a theme to all cards of the same number, as well as to all cards in the same suit. In this book, each number represents a Mythic Role, one of the archetypes who walk within the deck. For example, all the number five cards are The Warrior and the sevens are The Noble. Each suit then gives an action for that Role: "Promise," "Gambit," "Folly," or "Triumph." Every Role has one of each, producing a combination such as "Trickster's Gambit" or "Hermit's Folly." The full list of these names is shown here.

Ace = The Hunter	Eight = The Hermit
Two = The Lover	Nine = The Dancer
Three = The Healer	Ten = The Magician
Four = The Smith	Jack = The Trickster
Five = The Warrior	Queen = The Lady
Six = The Singer	King = The Sovereign
Seven = The Noble	
Clubs = Promise	Spades = Folly
Diamonds = Gambit	Hearts = Triumph

An Important Note on Gender

While some readers might think of Roles such as the Warrior or the Blacksmith as being male, they are not. Warriors and smiths have always been female, male, and neither; in this deck, they are very specifically available to any gender. Even the Queen cards as "the Lady" represent a figure of pure luck and chance with no gender, and the King as "the Sovereign" can be a ruler who is female, male, or other. Please read all of these Roles as whichever gender you wish.

Stories and Transformation

The card meanings are written in a specific way. The first page of each number is an overview of the Mythic Role, such as "the Hunter" or "the Healer." The four cards for that Role will then be listed in the order of: Clubs (Promise), Diamonds (Gambit), Spades (Folly), and Hearts (Triumph).

Each individual card then starts with a title, keywords, and a short story. This story does something very important: traditional playing card divination has only brief definitions, so by including these tales the pack is instead transformed into a book in your hand that has many characters, struggles, and colourful places. When readers pick up the cards they could meet masked street heroes and their deadly enemies in Venice, students of science choosing their prize, or a phoenix made of stars finding its way home. The plain pip designs remind us of richer adventures.

This isn't an unusual idea! "Transformation" playing card decks (popular throughout America and Europe in the 1800s) took the pips on a card, for example six red hearts, and drew a picture around them that turned them into the angry faces of six enemy warriors. By illustrating the whole deck this way, artists created a scenario on each card. The short stories in this book are there to do the same thing but in words. Though optional, they will add a lot of fun and adventure to the experience of reading with the deck.

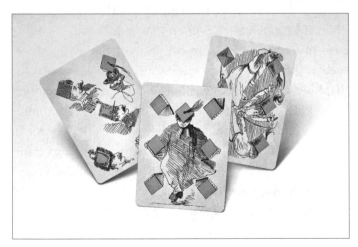

After the story section the divinatory meaning of the card is given in detail and the differences that "Promise," "Gambit," and the other suits bring to the Roles are explained. We then look at how the meaning often relates to real life, as well as how it might change in combination with other cards.

While the meanings are modern and useful, the stories and Mythic Roles are deliberately separate from our daily reality. Cards have been with us since the 1300s and there was a big resurgence of both gambling and divination in the medieval period using cards, dice, and other forms. The stories in this book are historical, magical, fantastic, and mundane. In order to bring to light the centuries of legend and storytelling over card tables (and help us speak to our own subconscious and intuition as we use them) they feature warriors and generals, dragons and elemental spirits, schoolteachers and young thieves. The essential lessons of people exploring their place in the world have not changed since the time of nobles and blacksmiths (both roles are still with us today, in fact) and so the themes are deliberately set outside the scientific modern world.

That final section of the page also talks about the wisdom that each card brings to a journey which runs all the way through the deck, Aces to Tens.

The Journey Through the Roles

In some systems of divination there is a path of discovery the reader can take from the first card to the last. In tarot this has become known as "the Fool's Journey" through the major arcana. The Fool begins in innocence, encounters the challenges of the World, and grows to master all aspects of life.

The playing card deck also has a journey and lessons to be learned. In it, the Hunter starts alone before meeting others in society as the Lover and the Healer, acts in the world as the Smith and the Warrior, wrestles with fame and power as the Singer and the Noble, looks within to find a new way of being as the Hermit and the Dancer, and brings together everything learned along the way as the Magician.

This path is called the Magician's Journey, because every lesson makes the Hunter (and also the reader) more capable at meeting the challenges of life. These are also exactly the same as the skills which make a magician better at magic: strength of character, knowledge of the self, exploring how we interact with the world—all these things go into making a person truly capable and powerful.

The wisdom of each Role will be covered in the section just before the definitions of the four cards of that number as well as in the pages for each card. Following the Journey can help you to better understand the energy of each card during divination and to bring their power into your own life.

Buying Your Own Decks of Cards

There is a huge variety of playing card designs available today. Just as tarot decks are created in all the themes you can imagine, so too are playing cards: with art featuring gold leaf, fine paintings, nature, old-fashioned parchment, animals, modern computer graphics—there are thousands of versions available.

They can also be extremely cheap to buy, which is an important part of why this system was written. My previous book gave readers a full experience of divination with the magical correspondences of the elements using only normal dice. Just like dice, playing cards are cheap and easy to find, convenient to carry with you, and do not look like occult objects if you wish to use them in public. These fifty-two cards with their centuries of history and lore are available much more cheaply and easily than other decks, and you may be delighted at just how many designs there are to choose from.

Using This System with a Deck of Tarot Cards

If you already own a tarot deck, you can use it with this system as well. Simply put some of the tarot cards to one side so that the remainder fit the playing card order. To do this, remove all of the major arcana and the four Pages. This will leave you with Aces to Tens, Knight (Jack), Queen, and King. The suit of Swords are Spades (from the Italian for "sword," *spada*), Wands are Clubs, Coins are Diamonds, and Cups are Hearts. Using tarot cards works even more easily with Marseille-type decks, where the minor arcana already show playing card pips instead of a fully illustrated scene on each card.

But of course, the original feel of this system comes from a plain set of normal Poker-style cards, not tarot. Playing cards are cheap, easy to buy, and have their own history of excitement, chance, and conflict. Even if you already own tarot, try using a deck of modern playing cards and note the differences.

A Summary Table of Card Meanings

You can use this table to find the basic keywords that each card represents, for quick readings. For more developed answers you can go to the main page for that card. (They are in this order in the book, and page numbers are also available on the contents page and in the appendix).

Card	Title	Story	Keywords
Ace of Clubs	Hunter's Promise	Alanna Hunts the Dragon	A New Beginning, Personal Goals, Focus
Ace of Diamonds	Hunter's Gambit	Sev Sees the Target	An Opportunity, Test of Skill, Going All In
Ace of Spades	Hunter's Folly	Nikolai Finds Only Death	Disaster, Ruthlessness, Sudden Change
Ace of Hearts	Hunter's Triumph	Sophia Claims the Silver Arrow	Joy, Gaining Your Heart's Desire, Strong Success
Two of Clubs	Lover's Promise	Aisling Walks in Autumn Leaves	Hope, Romance and Fantasy; Comfort
Two of Diamonds	Lover's Gambit	Lela Steals a Kiss	Emotional Risk, Agreements, Contracts
Two of Spades	Lover's Folly	Rickard Floats Downstream	Heartbreak, Argument, Angry Words
Two of Hearts	Lover's Triumph	Yelen Looks to the Stars	Love, Partners, Intimacy

Card	Title	Story	Keywords
Three of Clubs	Healer's Promise	Hanna and the Soldier	Moral Decisions, Compassion, Principles
Three of Diamonds	Healer's Gambit	Angelique Receives a Gift	Gift, Good Deeds, Assistance
Three of Spades	Healer's Folly	Peter's Poor Excuses	Exhaustion, Undeserved Guilt, Overwork
Three of Hearts	Healer's Triumph	Hazel Brought to Judgement	Gratitude, Recognition, Teamwork
Four of Clubs	Smith's Promise	Dinri and the Shining City	Long-term Work, Planning, Patience
Four of Diamonds	Smith's Gambit	Fiona's Masterpiece	Creation, Skilled Work, Planned Change
Four of Spades	Smith's Folly	Nell Clings to the Window	Greed, Inertia, Obsession
Four of Hearts	Smith's Triumph	Old Fu Eats a Pear	Harvest, Order, Fairness

Five of Clubs	Warrior's Promise	Temir of the Three Chiefs	Conflict, Necessary Opposition, Resistance
Five of Diamonds	Warrior's Gambit	Elena on the Burning Sands	Courage, Overcoming Fear, Taking Action
Five of Spades	Warrior's Folly	Ferghus, Shunned And Alone	Acting Rashly, Dishonorable Actions, Shame
Five of Hearts	Warrior's Triumph	Ambassador Levan's Game	Victory, Beating Stronger Opponents, Safety
Six of Clubs	Singer's Promise	Claire Reads a Secret	Communication, Written Messages, Being Understood
Six of Diamonds	Singer's Gambit	The Lady of the Forest	Performance, Outward Appearances, Being Seen
Six of Spades	Singer's Folly	Jenny Buys Another Round	Celebration, Holiday, Care-free Enjoyment
Six of Hearts	Singer's Triumph	Lissa Sings of Love and Sorrow	Persuasion, Fame, Glamor

Card	Title	Story	Keywords
Seven of Clubs	Noble's Promise	Lady Mapenzi Faces the Storm	Home, Fair Dealing, Contentment
Seven of Diamonds	Noble's Gambit	Omorede is Not Alone	Friendship, Loyalty, Recognising Debts
Seven of Spades	Noble's Folly	Tatiana, Queen of the World	Ego, Prejudice, Injustice
Seven of Hearts	Noble's Triumph	Dalton's Empty Advice	Searching for Answers, Continuing Responsibility, Restlessness
Eight of Clubs	Hermit's Promise	Sara Reaches the Empty Sky	Travel, Peace, Escape
Eight of Diamonds	Hermit's Gambit	Hedda Speaks to The Ancestors	Mental Effort, Clarity, Ignoring Interruptions
Eight of Spades	Hermit's Folly	The Emerald Mask Repaid	Isolation, Overthinking, Prioritizing Thoughts over Deeds
Eight of Hearts	Hermit's Triumph	The Phoenix and the Stars	Reconciliation, New Knowledge, Returning

Card	Story	Meaning
Nine of Clubs	Dancer's Promise	Adelise Listens Within	Intuition, Connection, Avoiding Danger
Nine of Diamonds	Dancer's Gambit	Anja Enters the Cave	Cycles, Habits, Burdens
Nine of Spades	Dancer's Folly	Mara, Lost in Beauty	Illusion, Self-Deception, Imbalance
Nine of Hearts	Dancer's Triumph	Hyun-Ki Chases His Master	Paths, Easy Progress, Harmony
Ten of Clubs	Magician's Promise	Jess Throws an Acorn	Balance, Self-Discipline Fairness
Ten of Diamonds	Magician's Gambit	Isla and the Four Spirits	Juggling, Reducing Chaos, Applying Knowledge
Ten of Spades	Magician's Folly	Mother Olivia's Magic	Simple Tasks, Avoiding Arrogance, Routine Work
Ten of Hearts	Magician's Triumph	Alanna Faces the Dragon	Mastery, Completion, Success Through Learning

Card	Title	Story	Keywords
Jack of Clubs	Trickster's Promise	Sabina Betrayed	Lies, Betrayal, Worthless Assurances
Jack of Diamonds	Trickster's Gambit	Beth Meets a Good Dog	Unexpected Lessons, Risks for Large Gains
Jake of Spades	Trickster's Folly	Harry's Run Cut Short	Honesty, Justice, Exposing Liars
Jake of Hearts	Trickster's Triumph	Leo Plays in the Woods	Jackpot, Great Assistance, Unconventional Routes
Queen of Clubs	Lady's Promise	Agnetha and the Firefly	Temptation, Excitement, Future Possibilities
Queen of Diamonds	Lady's Gambit	Francois Flips a Coin	Pure Chance
Queen of Spades	Lady's Folly	Elin Climbs the Tower	Bad Luck
Queen of Hearts	Lady's Triumph	Sawyer and the Faery	Good Luck

King of Clubs	Sovereign's Promise	Xavier's Prison	Security, Benevolent Institutions, Fulfilling Promises
King of Diamonds	Sovereign's Gambit	Matthew And the Baker	Money, Diplomacy, Professional Services
King of Spades	Sovereign's Folly	Calum Breaks the Old Rules	Authority, Tradition, Inflexibility
King of Hearts	Sovereign's Triumph	Vettorio's Canvas	Help from a Master, Allies, Success in Traditional Ways

CHAPTER TWO

READING THE CARDS,
OR "DEALING A HAND"

Reading with this system is a little different to other types of card divination you may be familiar with, such as tarot. Instead of laying out cards in a spread or pattern, you can deal the playing cards as though you are starting a game.

The typical number of cards in a reading will either be one, two, or five. If you are using just one card, then the answer for the whole reading is given on the page for that result. If you are using two or more, the reading is performed differently. Several of the cards can be read together and have equal importance for the final answer.

Let's look at how each of these can work, and then at some examples of the actual answers we can get from the cards in each format.

One-card Reading

This is drawing a single card when you need a quick answer to a specific question.

Look at the definition, and also the suit to determine how lucky the card appears to be in general. Many of the Spades cards will carry a warning about events, whereas a Heart card usually suggests a good outcome regardless of the specific number. (We'll look at these meanings in detail in a later section.)

Two-card Reading

Shuffle the deck, and then take the two cards from the top. It doesn't matter which one comes first; you can hold both in your hand and shuffle them around. Both cards are equally important in the reading, and both apply to the reading. There isn't a fixed definition for "Card 1 means this, Card 2 means that;" instead, the two meanings interact with each other.

Five-card Reading

The format for reading with five cards is very different from the one- and two-card readings: it is structured like a game of five-card stud poker. (In recent times the most popular type of poker has become Texas No Limit Hold 'Em, but older forms from the 1800s used five cards instead of seven and revealed more of the cards to everyone, reducing the ability to bluff. Stud poker works very well as a format for divination!)

The first two cards are dealt together. These give the reading's *current situation*. You can move these in any order after you have picked them up and held them in your hand, just as you can for the two-card reading earlier. Place the first two face up in front of you and work out what you think they mean before moving on to the third card. In some versions of stud, the first card is face down to everyone else and the second one up, but there are no other players to hide the results from in this reading so you can look at both face up immediately.

The third card is then drawn and placed to the right of the pair (again, face up). This card shows an aspect which is coming to *challenge* the situation, such as an external influence or person. The third is often called "Third Street" in poker.

The fourth card is drawn and again placed to the right of the current three. It represents forces and ideas which will *help* the client. In poker, this card is called "the Turn" or "Fourth Street." It often turns the direction of the hand in unexpected ways. In divination, it can offer a way past an issue that seemed hopeless moments before.

The fifth and final card shows an *action* or route that you can take to resolve the situation for the best results. It can therefore be a suggestion to be bold or a warning to play it safe. (Card five is called the "River" or "Fifth Street" in poker, where it is decisive in whether the hand is a success or earlier promises haven't worked out. If you just needed one more card for a combination, it's this one which sometimes "sells you down the river.")

A typical five-card spread is therefore:

1, 2 = Current situation, any order

3 = Challenges

4 = Helping influences

5 = A suggested action for best results

Now let's look at some examples of readings using each of these formats.

One-card Reading Example

A friend asked whether she should take a risk and apply for a job with more responsibility. She talked a little about two options, listing details about money and travel. Drawing just one card revealed the Nine of Clubs, "Dancer's Promise."

This is the card of intuition, of walking through life really connected to your inner self. All her discussion had been about technical things, but a job is something that will affect you quite deeply and you will do for hours every day. How did she feel about the two options on an intuitive level, not just around practical concerns like money? At this point, she admitted there was something making her very uncomfortable about the riskier job, but she had been trying to ignore it by looking at the benefits. Intuition— especially a flowing connection like the Dancer has—can be a useful and revealing tool for looking at problems from another direction.

One-card Reading Example 2

A client was worried about keeping some news from everyone. The card drawn was the Seven of Diamonds, "Noble's Gambit."

The message was very clearly, "Lean on your friends and family; they will support you." The Noble calls on the loyalty of those around them and pays it back through good and responsible actions. When they make a gambit, they use friendship to help them win based on the loyalty they have earned previously. The client's friends would be part of the solution.

The client decided to open up to those close to him. He could even think of examples of when he'd been supportive of them in exactly this way previously! After talking it over, he was sure they'd understand, and that this would be easily resolved with the help of others.

Two-card Reading Example

A client asked about what would happen in the next week. She didn't have anything particular in mind, only to look at what the future would bring. The two cards drawn were the Three of Diamonds ("Healer's Gambit") and the Jack of Clubs ("Trickster's Promise").

The Three of Diamonds is usually a wonderful card to see, meaning receiving a nice gift or doing a good deed. Unfortunately, the Jack of Clubs reverses all of that! A Trickster's Promise is a lie, and changes the meaning of any other card it is paired with. In this case it said that she shouldn't trust any offer which looked too good to be true in the next few days, especially if it was a free gift.

These changes in meaning are only possible when multiple cards are linked in the reading and are a big part of what the two- and five-card readings add to the divination. The answer isn't "You will have a good experience and a bad one" separately, the meanings are added together before giving the final answer.

Two-card Reading Example 2

A friend of mine asked about their relationship. (Every good divination system should have plenty to say about romantic relationships!) The cards were the Two of Clubs ("Lover's Promise") and the Four of Spades ("Smith's Folly").

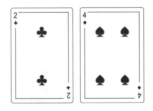

The first one of these is very simple and an excellent card for romance. It tells us to trust that the best future can happen, to be gentle with each other, and to believe that loved ones can be genuine.

The second card is less positive. Spades are the "Folly" of each Role and usually give a warning. This one tells us what happens when a Blacksmith gets too caught up in the process of their work, losing sight of the end goal and just working all day, becoming greedy, not taking care of their other duties while they pursue this one thing.

Taken together, these two cards told my friend that they should first relax and believe that a good outcome was still possible. She should remember the best and most romantic days, and try to make more of them. At the same time, she needed to look clearly at the important things within the relationship that they'd both stopped doing as daily life got in the way. Inertia and routine tasks can be boring and are the total opposite of the very hopeful Lover's Promise. The two cards together said that the romance was being stopped by the Folly.

(There's a happy ending to this one, as they made excellent choices and it worked out better than other friends or I could have guessed!)

Five-card Reading Example

A client wanted to know how to advance at work. They weren't happy in the work environment, and there was conflict with their boss.

The five-card reading started with the first two cards:

1. Ace of Hearts (Hunter's Triumph)
2. Nine of Diamonds (Dancer's Gambit)

These two are dealt together and can be moved into any order in the hand after being picked up and examined. They mean: gaining your heart's desire, and cycles and habits. The first is a very positive card, the second is neutral. Looking at them together, we see that they say, "This concerns something personally important for you, and there's a cycle involved."

We discussed how this message could relate to their work. They said that they certainly weren't getting their heart's desire there; every time they seemed to be making progress, they would be ignored and find themselves back at the beginning again. The fact that this had happened repeatedly was exactly what had caused them to look for new solutions now.

The third card shows a challenge in the situation, and it was:

3. Seven of Spades (Noble's Folly)

This Folly is the ego or prejudice of the Noble, who should know better. Like many Spades cards, this one is quite negative.

The client said that they became defensive and flustered at work whenever circumstances made it look as though they weren't on top of things. They hated the idea that they were doing a bad job but would then act in ways which didn't look very reliable (and made everything worse). This behavior fit the reading quite well: a repeated habit of letting their sensitive self-image stop them achieving their desired goal.

The fourth card is a helpful outside influence:

4. King of Diamonds (Sovereign's Gambit)

This usually means someone more powerful than you who will be spending money, or someone who has money who will be exercising their authority. In a work situation, it is often a boss or person representing a large institution. It is very good that this appeared in the fourth place as a helpful force—it might mean there would be an opportunity for a raise, or at the very least, the attention of a senior colleague who could improve things and be supportive.

The fifth card in this reading is an action which the client should take to make the best outcome happen:

5. Ace of Diamonds (Hunter's Gambit)

This card is full of decisive action already, even if it hadn't appeared in fifth place (an action for the person to take). The instruction is to go all-in and commit to something that could have a big payoff. Aces are concerned with just one prize, and much like the Ace of Hearts earlier in the reading, that prize usually has deep personal meaning for the client.

Combined with the earlier card which showed that cycles are part of the problem, the overall reading says "Use the opportunity that is coming up to escape the cycle and move on. Gather all your resources and take a risk if you want to progress to better things."

I heard from the client later on, who said they were much happier! Their next week had been good, and the month after that was better. They managed to stop assuming that any criticism of their department's work was about them personally and volunteered for the responsibility they wanted, even though it felt like a scary jump into the unknown. The tense moment of going all-in is a joy for the character in the short story on the Ace of Diamonds page but can be very difficult in real life! Sometimes a suggestion from the cards is all we need to realize that this big risk can still be an option if our desire is strong enough.

How to Interpret Unexpected
Combinations in the Five-card Reading

As soon as a system assigns meanings to the order that cards are drawn in (for example, positions three, four, and five in the five-card reading), unusual combinations of a card and its place can arise. A totally beneficial outcome can appear in a position which indicates danger, or two completely opposite cards can be paired together by the format of the reading. This section explains some of these situations.

Positive Cards in the "Challenge" Third Card Place

What happens when the third card, a problem for us, is one with a very positive meaning? If you draw the Jack of Hearts, it means "Winning the Jackpot"—that hardly sounds like a problem!

The key to any unexpected combination is to look at how the basic definition could be made into a good or bad thing for you. In this case, someone else is taking the jackpot shortcut. The action will be fast so you are short on time to beat them. Read in the "Challenge" position, the message becomes "this card is happening without you—act now!"

Negative Cards in the Fourth "Helpful Influence"
or Fifth "Action for Best Outcome" Places

If a position is supposed to help you but the card is a negative one such as the Queen of Spades (Lady's Folly, meaning very bad luck) this can be confusing.

There are two main approaches to a negative card in this place. The card could be saying "Bad luck is happening, so you need to accept it. The way to help yourself is to plan so that this doesn't affect you. The helpful part here is the knowledge that it's coming." Alternatively, it might be "What appears to be bad luck actually isn't. Don't be angry if things don't go your way—this will turn out to have been helping you later." Or, if the first cards are strongly about somebody else, the helpful news may be that they are the ones receiving the bad luck. Card readers are used to the idea that very extreme cards can appear as nice influences; intuition or even some detail of the client's situation can help us to find the key to a puzzling combination.

Positive and Negative Cards Appearing Together
(For Example, As Cards One and Two)

A good example of this particular conflict is the Jack of Hearts and Jack of Spades in a pair (Trickster's Triumph and Trickster's Folly). One means successfully carrying out a trick, and the other is about having the truth exposed so that you can't do that. How do you reconcile these two?

When we combine two cards, we need to tell a story. The answer to that story isn't always the same each time. We can also do this when trying to see how any two cards could come together.

The Trickster teaches unexpected wisdom to others. They have unique views that surprise people. Paired with a card that means "the truth is clearly seen," the combined meaning suggests that their unusual tricks become accepted as superior.

A Triumph card means that success is guaranteed. This combination doesn't mean taking a risk and getting caught out; it says that the truth and justice of the Folly means that the unconventional approach of the Triumph was always the right thing to do.

There are many cards which appear to fight each other when they first appear in a pair but can be found to be supportive or illuminating if we take a little time to see how they could cooperate.

More Examples of Card Pairs

Making a reading from more than one card can be difficult for new readers, so here are some more examples.

Eight of Clubs and King of Hearts (Hermit's Promise and Sovereign's Triumph): To gain peace and a retreat from daily chaos, look for a master who will give you advice.

Ace of Diamonds and King of Spades (Hunter's Gambit and Sovereign's Folly): The Ace is a test of skill, going all in to hit a target. The King is the negative effects of inflexible traditions. You are therefore being blocked from pursuing your dream by an institution that won't bend the rules.

Two of Hearts and Eight of Hearts (Lover's Triumph and Hermit's Triumph): The Two means success in love, and the Eight is returning after being away having learned valuable lessons. This is therefore the only combination where you're allowed to phone your ex.

Four of Hearts and Five of Clubs (Smith's Triumph and Warrior's Promise): The Smith brings a reward after a time of peacefully working hard, but the Warrior promises resistance and conflict. Why would you ever resist a peaceful reward? Well, the Smith's Triumph is the long-term and predictable ending of some work. Sometimes, the way things are traditionally done is too restrictive or isn't the best way for you. You might also disagree with the reward that appears after so much work. (This turned out to be that the client really didn't like the ending of his long-running television show. What can I say? Sometimes the cards just read the person's strongest emotions in the moment!)

Playing Against Fate

A unique way to perform readings is in the format of a card game. Instead of dealing the cards to yourself and then turning them over, you can deal the first card to yourself and the second card to a different pile in front of you, as though it was to an opponent. The third card then goes to you again, giving you two in total, and the fourth card gives another to your opponent. (The opponent's cards all stay face down; ignore them for now).

You then pick up your own cards and interpret the reading as normal. If you are using a five-card reading, this means putting out a total of ten cards but only looking at the five in front of you.

There is now a way that you can interact with the new line of "opponent" cards, although it is entirely optional. The other player in the game of cards is Fate, who offers you the chance to change your luck. When you have dealt your own cards and looked at them, the answers might not be what you want. In fact, they might be exactly the opposite of what you had hoped for! In that case, there is something you can do: pay to see your opponent's cards.

Paying to See involves paying a small coin of very low value (of any type suitable to where you live). This should have very little real-world cost. You must take this coin and place it on the table between the two rows of cards. It is now spent, and you may turn over the opponent's cards to see what they are.

The coin really does have to be spent—take it and put it in a lucky place of water, such as a fountain, wishing well, or river. Alternatively, you can drop it in the street for someone to find as a lucky coin when they walk along. Paying to see Fate's cards really must cost you this coin; the process is not free.

Now that you've paid, you can see the cards. If Fate's hand is so good that you would prefer it to your own, you can also *Change Your Luck*.

To do this, pay a second coin in the same way and draw an extra card. You can now take Fate's hand and discard your own. This buys you the cards in Fate's hand to use instead of your original answer, but there is a catch: this is not the fate that will come to you if the current situation continues. If you want this second outcome, as well as paying the two coins you will have to take real steps to make this new reading come about. That is where the extra card comes in. That card is the action required to get away from your current fate and move in the direction of the one you have bought. You cannot simply pay coins and change your fate—you must work to reach the new goal using the extra single card as your route.

Remember that all of this is optional. You could deal only to yourself, or deal for the opponent but ignore that line completely. You can pay one coin and then stop after the step of seeing the other cards, or you can go all the way and pay another coin to buy the hand instead of the one you were dealt. You then draw the extra card as your clue on how to achieve it.

Dealing only to yourself without playing against Fate is equally good, but some have found that this optional format adds an aspect to the divination that brings the magic of card games and history to the table.

If you do not wish to use the coins, there is another way to engage with these optional rules: Jokers.

Jokers

Joker cards first appeared in 1857, for the game of euchre. They are very distinctive personalities and art in any deck! They do not form part of the normal divination here, but you can include them in your pack if you ever consider *Changing Your Luck* as in the previous section.

If a Joker comes up in your reading, immediately put it to one side and draw a new card to replace it. When you have all of your cards, the Joker can then be used instead of coins to *Pay to See* and *Change Your Luck* without spending an actual coin. One Joker replaces both coins for these, although you can still choose to do neither or to stop after only *Paying to See*. The choice is up to you; the Joker simply makes it free and removes the need for coins.

No Reversals

One distinctive part of interpretation in this system is that there are no reversed readings. Cards cannot appear upside down, because many modern playing cards are mirrored.

For example, you can't tell which way up the Four of Diamonds is when you see it, up and down are identical.

This mirroring is deliberate. Early versions of the court cards were not symmetrical—under the familiar head and upper body, the figures used to have legs and feet! The design was changed when it was realised that players were turning these cards right side up in their hands, which gave away to their opponents that they had good cards. (Amazingly, it took over three hundred years to realise this). As late as the 1800s there were still decks in the old style. Even when a pip card (such as the Three of Spades) has one pip in the middle that has to be either up or down, players don't rotate these cards in their hand. Card numbers are printed in the corners and do not draw attention to the direction the central pip faces.

For all these reasons, reversals are not a part of playing card divination.

Other Card Spreads

The cards can be used in the formats given here or in more traditional tarot spreads. The classic three-card spread showing past, present, and future works very well—each card is read individually and related to only that position instead of shuffling the three together.

Other spread position meanings could be: hopes and fears, choices to be made, the influence of friends, or what romantic events could be in the future. Your cards can use these methods just as easily as the systems given earlier. Begin with the one, two, or five in this book, and also experiment with your own spreads and see which work best for you.

One alternative style in particular is to read five cards without using the place meanings for challenges, helpful influence, and action but instead adding each new meaning to an ongoing story. Speak out loud as you add new cards and try to bring their meanings into the existing mix as though it's a conversation: "The main message is this, and this. This third card is added to it. There will be this fourth influence. Hmm, I want more detail. What does the fifth say and how does that change the others?"

This method of reading can be quite advanced; it can be difficult to balance five messages if you haven't had practice with two-card readings first. It is similar to systems such as Lenormand where many cards are used at once—in fact, there is even a famous Lenormand spread, the Grand Tableau, that uses all 36 cards in one big reading! In it, the cards dealt in positions close to the one chosen to represent you are more relevant, and those farther away don't apply. This isn't as useful with a standard 52-card deck, as it leads to a lot of ignored cards, but holding five cards in a fan in your hand can provide a lot of information to which your intuition may be applied.

Your ideas don't have to be limited to only changing the number of cards you draw. One historical method that has been recorded is to drop a six-sided die onto the four King or Queen cards, and note which one it lands on. The number on the dice then tells you the outcome (even numbers only, roll again if it comes up an odd number). I'm fond of dice divination, so I like this mixing of the two. It is a great example of just how varied playing card divination has been in the past.

The deck is yours and the games you play with it are yours as well. Take the spreads in this section as a beginning and find the ways that work best for you. Start simple and find a place that you are comfortable with.

Remembering the Definitions

"Folly? Singer? Promise? Help!" Although the ideas in this system are part of a universal human experience, they're still new to every reader and learning all the definitions at once can be intimidating. The best way to start is to read all of the next section in order: this will help you see the journey that the Magician takes, from one person to two, to many, from ideals to worldly power and then to inner wisdom.

You will also learn the suits easily. Clubs are first and Promise what's to come, Diamonds are money being gambled (Gambit), Spades are the dangerous or unlucky suit that shows the flaws of each Role (Folly), and Hearts are your friend because they show success (Triumph). If you read the next section and also look up the individual pages when you try your first few readings, you will quickly find that you remember the name and Role for each. The stories also help to bring the important parts of the meaning to mind.

Now let's look at the meanings of each card in detail.

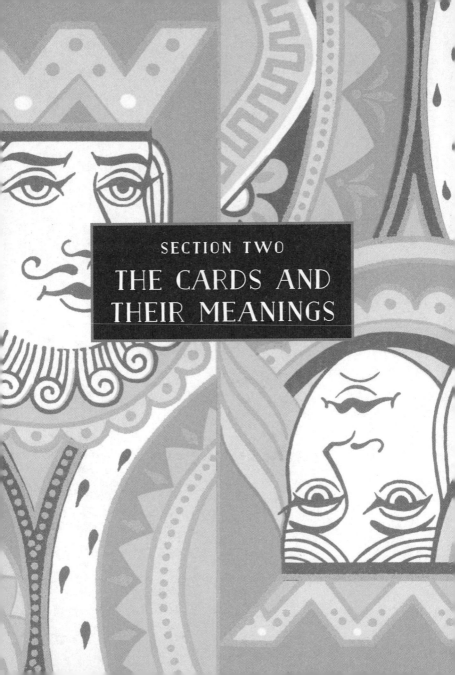

SECTION TWO

THE CARDS AND THEIR MEANINGS

CHAPTER THREE

THE PIP CARDS

The Aces and number cards all represent concepts you can experience yourself. They move from the simple life of the Hunter, forming links to wider society and finding internal growth, to the mastery of the Magician. The Tens are the end of this personal journey, and the Court cards afterward show a different set of external forces.

In this section each Role will get its own explanation, followed by an in-depth look at the four cards within it. The numbers and suits increase in the natural progression of meanings: the early Promise, using the skill as Gambit, finding the dangers in Folly, and succeeding as Triumph. Read the stories to get a feel for the personality of each card, and then use the detailed definitions for readings.

THE ACES: THE HUNTER

This first Role includes several traditional meanings of the number one: a single person with a single idea, not yet distracted by the larger concerns of society.

The Hunter travels alone, moving toward their goal while maintaining complete focus. Their life is very simple, they look along the arrow and see only the target. Worrying about events at home or how to interact with others won't help them catch their prize, so those are ignored while the hunt is on.

Many Roles later in the deck are based on relationships with the wider world, but the Hunter is not interested in that. They have a main hunt which takes all of their attention. Whoever you are reading for, this goal is always something that the subject of the reading truly needs—it goes beyond idly wanting it and is instead connected to their deepest passions. (If the person is unhappy because they can't seem to find a single thing to be that passionate about, then the goal is often the search itself until it is successful).

In terms of the Magician's Journey through the deck, there is nothing else to concentrate on at this time. Everything outside of your target is a blank canvas. This is a place of beginnings and seeking something which feels more important than other events.

The Hunter may be the first Role, but their personality is not new or childlike—they believe that they have the right to exist, want things for themselves, and pursue those things even if it means taking a risk. They must already believe that they deserve to take up space in the world and have their own desires independent of other people. This isn't something everyone finds easy to do, but it is necessary if they are to be a Hunter.

The second skill they need is to focus intensely on a single task—again, a difficult thing for many of us! The strength of demand from the Ace encourages the reader to find a way to do both.

As the Hunter moves through the deck, they will learn that we all have to reach out to others, to make more complicated decisions, and to find different ways of living. None of this comes into play for the Aces which are too primal and too immediate. They help the Hunter to focus only on the prize.

ACE OF CLUBS:
HUNTER'S PROMISE
"ALANNA HUNTS THE DRAGON"

A New Beginning, Personal Goals, Focus

Alanna moved quietly through the forest. The light was warm and golden, with soft shadows from the many trees which surrounded her, but she kept her eyes on the ground. Tracks in the soil showed that small animals had passed this way earlier—and had then run quickly home again.

The young mage stopped to crouch at the edge of a clearing, glad that she'd changed her formal blue robes for the brown scouting clothes that were easier to move in. Searching the area carefully, she thought back to the conversation that had started it all.

The leader of the Academy had called her to his office. It was a room she'd never been to before, furnished in rich wood and with many books on shelves, but he captured her interest away from them with his first words:

"There is a message from the islands in the far West. A Dragon has been found."

The shock quickly passed, and Alanna felt only a warm certainty. Her time with them was over and this would be the beginning of the rest of her life. She answered without hesitating.

"I will seek it."

The leader regarded Alanna with a serious expression. "You have earned the right to do so, but … are you sure? It means leaving your studies and this land, being focused on nothing but the pursuit. You would be travelling alone."

"I know. I am ready."

She stood before him calm and determined, and he saw in her face that the walls of the school were confining to her now, and she wanted to be out in the world. After a few moments he nodded sharply. "Very well, then. It passed through the Southern Forest on its way to the islands, you could start there."

She was filled with joy as she prepared for the journey. Mages sought Dragons for many reasons but in every case it led to knowledge, accomplishment and mastery. Alanna shouldered her pack and stood for a moment in the doorway, taking a last look at the study room which had been her home.

The next day she was in the forest where the Dragon had been sighted. The clearing was silent as she moved slowly on, checking for signs. Suddenly the ground in front of her showed the huge clawed print that she had hoped for—and her vision blurred. A new feeling rose in the mage's chest. She felt connected to the mysterious creature that she was to chase, tied to it now, and knew that across time and many lands she would not stop travelling until they met. Through orchards, and royal palaces and … starbirds in the night sky?

The images slowly faded, leaving her breathless. She sensed immediately that it had been a true vision. Instead of feeling *afraid or cautious, it only made her more eager. This Hunt was on now, wherever it led, and every step from this point would bring freedom and discovery.*

Aces (and the number one) in card divination often mean new beginnings, or the most fundamental version of a theme. The Promise cards of each number also mean a beginning, a time full of potential when all good things could arrive in the future and nothing is yet decided. The Ace of Clubs (Hunter's Promise) is therefore the very start of a new journey. By coincidence, in the game of Hearts, the players also begin with the lowest Clubs card, just as the Roles do here.

Ace cards are potent symbols that have always drawn the attention of players and audiences. When they appear in these readings they represent subjects close to the heart of the reader, never trivial or small matters. The Hunter's personality is the same: their goal is particularly meaningful to them and they don't look around at anything else. The Promise of this card is the future that the Hunter can eventually achieve, of tracking and gaining an important prize. This journey is taken alone, and the Hunter must go to seek their quarry with great determination.

If you receive this card then it is time to examine any distractions around you and deliberately put them aside. Don't let your energy go to anything except hunting the real prize. A project will be of great importance to you. Hunter's Promise tells you to prepare well, to plan, and to know the goal that you seek. Part of that planning is to look again at what is really important in your life.

This is a card of new beginnings, but it can also relate to an existing situation. Often the message is "Right! You know that thing you've been delaying on? Time to finally start it and not give up until it's done. It'll be an adventure." Although the topic the card relates to is usually the first one you think of (because it feels the most important) it can still be scary to follow that call—there may be good reasons that you haven't made a proper attempt yet! However, the Hunter has an urgent energy and certainty which overrides any doubts. The appearance of Hunter's Promise in a reading means that you are going to want to drop everything else to do this.

While the idea of a lone figure going on a journey may remind readers of the tarot's Fool card, Hunter's Promise is quite different. Instead of carefree wandering, this is the first step on a directed and planned journey with a goal at the end. The Hunter is not as innocent or naïve as the Fool. They may not be paying much attention to events on either side, but their ability to focus in on the main goal is admirable.

ACE OF DIAMONDS:
HUNTER'S GAMBIT
"SEV SEES THE TARGET"

An Opportunity, Test of Skill, Going All In

As the crowd roared, Sev walked to the area where archers should stand. Everyone was here today to see the competition.

Excitement tingled in their gloved hands and they checked the bow before turning to wave to the many spectators. Straw targets were being replaced after the last round of shooting and moved a long distance down the range for the final attempt. That didn't matter. This was what all the training had been for, all the preparation.

This was the best moment, the few seconds before anything was decided when all the possibilities were still in play. Would the arrow hit or miss? Whose name would the crowd be calling at the end of the tournament? These hands will decide it, these eyes!

The breeze was soft, with no unexpected gusts. The sun shone onto the targets from above, bringing out their bright colours.

Sev slowly raised the bow and drew the arrow back to their cheek. The noise of the crowd faded away, but as the string was briefly held against skin, the mouth beneath it broke into a grin of joy.

Here we go—all or nothing! Only skill will decide.

Wishing there was a way to make the moment last forever, Sev was still smiling as their fingers carefully relaxed and the arrow leapt into flight.

The Gambit cards have two meanings: taking an action in the way that only this particular Role can, and taking a risk. They are the Role that says, "I'm going to leave the safety of the planning stage in favour of action, and it's not certain that I'll succeed." After the rising energy of the Promise card (which starts a journey and moves towards the world of action) the Gambit's energy sits on a peak, capable of falling to either side. It could succeed or fail. Your protection during this gamble is that each Role has a special skill and can win using the talents familiar to them.

For the Hunter, that skill is tracking and capturing prey. Their Gambit is to create a moment when the target will either be caught or get away. The Ace of Diamonds (and many Gambit cards) can be pictured spinning like a coin: "I'm all-in. Let's see where the arrow lands."

The idea of hunting animals is not a pleasant one in the modern day, but thankfully the Ace of Diamonds shows us that this is not what the Role of the Hunter means at all. It is instead about quests and goals, and this Ace does a good job of resembling a valuable red gem that you are reaching out to take.

This is a very exciting and positive result! Having the opportunity to solve something with a big gesture is often a good situation to be in. Where Hunter's Promise was the beginning of a solo journey, the Gambit is the intense moment that everything hangs in the balance, ready to fall one way or the other.

When this card appears, it is telling you to fully commit to one action. You should see your goal clearly and make an attempt. If you have been undecided on a topic, this message says, "Focus only on the target, and seize it." You must put distractions to the side and ignore the whole world except for the target in front of your arrow; crucially, you must also take action. Planning and focus are not enough— you have to actually take the risk. A Gambit is a card of action, and there is no prize to be gained if you hesitate.

The Hunter's prize has the power of an Ace, meaning that it is very important to the person seeking answers. With topics so significant, we can often be afraid to take a leap in case we fail. It requires a lot of certainty to commit this much to something which isn't guaranteed, and the Hunter (at this starting point on the journey) have only themselves to rely on. This means that they must find some self-acceptance, and belief in their own skills.

This card is guidance that you should commit now and stop holding the arrow back. Let it make its journey. You might miss this time, but you definitely won't hit the target if you stay on the line holding the bowstring instead of letting it do the work it was meant for.

ACE OF SPADES:
HUNTER'S FOLLY
"NIKOLAI FINDS ONLY DEATH"

Ruthlessness, Disaster, Sudden Change

Nikolai was a man who hunted innocents, and today it was to be a farmer's daughter. Others might have hesitated to take these jobs from the chief of a clan known for its evil deeds, but Nikolai had only coldness in his heart and a love of coin.

This child of one of these local families had simply seen too much, and now the killer had arrived from the city to find her. With the heavy sword gripped in his hand, he would complete this mission just like so many others. There was no chance that his target would escape him—the rest of the girl's family were away celebrating the harvest, which is how the unfortunate youth had become the only witness to the deed. Now she needed to be removed.

Nikolai stalked silently into the village. Evening shadows hid his dark clothes as he crept between buildings hunting the chosen victim. He found one dwelling set apart from the others—this is where she should be. Moonlight barely showed on the blackened metal of his terrible blade.

It was a fine plan, but that night fate was not with the dangerous stranger. His heart, already foul from past deeds and dead to emotion, did not have time to jump as the hiss of unseen arrows came from either side. The girl's cousins lowered their bows, satisfied that the ambush had worked.

One mistake of overconfidence was all it had taken, and all of Nikolai's luck had run out.

Traditionally, the Ace of Spades is the card of death. There are many reasons for this association, but the main one is that companies were not allowed to print this specific card unless the official duty fee had been paid. The penalties for counterfeiting decks were severe, and this Ace was the proof of guilt. It is also the reason that this card often has a more intricate design today than any other in the pack: when the laws were changed later to allow anyone to print cards, designers kept the more elaborate Ace of Spades.

A second connection with death comes from this Ace's association with war. Soldiers have carried this card in the belief that it was lucky, although in the twentieth century they also dropped copies of it into enemy territory, believing it to be deeply unlucky and intimidating to the enemy.

In traditional playing card divination, the black suits (Clubs, but especially Spades) are considered worse and given the more negative outcomes. The suit of Spades in this book follows that approach, as the Folly cards are usually each Role's weakness or danger that should be overcome in order to learn its lessons. In the case of the Hunter, the folly is often the result of believing that the target is the only thing that matters to the exclusion of other hazards nearby. The Hunter is so focused on their chosen prey that they don't see enemies closing in from either side.

It's easy to become obsessed when we focus on just one target for a long time. However, the world is bigger than that and has more areas for you to play in and responsibilities to maintain. The Hunter thinks they are in control and superior to their prey, but the Folly card says that this isn't true in this situation. Do not be arrogant about your abilities, or obsessed with too narrow a goal, because you are very vulnerable here. You are hunted instead, by an enemy you did not see when you were busy aiming at your own targets.

The Ace of Spades means ruthlessness, disaster, or a catastrophic loss. It stops all other plans and forces you to concentrate on itself. It is a card so significant that if it comes up during a reading, you should stop everything else and pay attention to it. There is a danger associated with failure of some kind, a very serious one that cannot be waved away. Instead, it must be vigorously defended against.

If the cards show Hunter's Folly in a way that is actually positive, it means you should be ruthless. Matters have turned serious and you need to come out on top. Stop your previous plan—looking only in a single direction will not save you. You must also check on all sides and find the hidden threats before they strike.

Part of the Folly of the Hunter who silently advances through the forest, bow drawn, is that to be stealthy enough to close in on a target, they must work alone. This card therefore says that one way to avoid this fate is to reach out to others for help.

The energy of all the Folly cards fall downwards from the previous sharp peak of the Gambit cards. This Ace is the fastest and most dangerous falling Folly. Despite this, it does not mean actual death—card readers perform a lot of readings, and if we died every time one card out of fifty-two appeared then there wouldn't be any of us left! It is merely a warning to start putting your defenses up, or you will be hit by change that you did not expect.

Change is not death. Change is life. As you grow you become a different person, leaving the past behind when it is right to do so. You should not be the same person you were five years ago, for example. There are all kinds of things in your life that you should want to end, including events you've been struggling with and long-term situations you don't feel you can move out of. This card allows all of that to happen.

In this way the Ace of Spades keeps to its historical double "lucky" and "unlucky" nature. It is a disastrous change to the current situation … but sometimes we need those changes or were even hoping for them.

ACE OF HEARTS:
HUNTER'S TRIUMPH
"SOPHIA CLAIMS THE SILVER ARROW"

Joy, Gaining Your Heart's Desire, Strong Success

Sophia stood in line and waited for the announcement.

"And now, the winner of the prize for Sciences, Sophia Marin!"

The circle of people filling the small bookshop cheered and clapped, as she approached the old man behind the desk. Shelves full of books towered around them on all sides—the most coveted works in the land, a treasury of medicine, philosophy, and knowledge. All those nights alone studying had been worth it. She had passed the examinations and impressed the judges, and finally the book would be hers.

The small figure of the owner looked up from behind his delicate glasses. "My congratulations! Your prize is, as we all know, any book of your choosing from my stock."

The old women and men held their breath. They were crowded into the shop around the polished shelves and piles of famous tomes, eager to hear her answer. Would she choose the Treatise on Mathematics, which was the size of a small table and required three people to lift it? With that, she would have professors visiting her to consult on all the theories of the day. Or maybe one of the oldest works, each sought by collectors from far lands, which she could sell for a fortune and immediately retire?

"I will choose ... that one." She pointed to the large book that had shone in her dreams all this time, with its golden cover. There was immediate confusion from the other people, muttering and sounds of disbelief. She couldn't mean it, surely?

"Uh ... are you certain? That one?"

"Oh yes. It is rare, is it not?"

"Well ... of course, the only one of its kind in the country, as far as I know. And very valuable ... I suppose."

"Then I shall take my reward."

The whispers from the assembled doctors and scholars faded back to respectful silence as the owner turned and lifted the book from its display case. On its cover was a golden pattern featuring a large silver arrow, and the title, One Thousand Folk Tales from Faraway Lands.

Sophia bowed her head respectfully to the old man and received the prize. Smiling joyfully, she hugged it to her chest as she walked out into the street. Unable to wait, the young woman leaned against a wall and opened the gold-edged pages to a random chapter ... falling deliciously into worlds of wonder.

The Triumph cards show a full success, a happy and glorious win. They come at the end of everything, after you have planned and hoped, taken a chance, and avoided the dangers. The Triumph is what happens when the Role functions perfectly and is proven wise and effective, reaching the final goal according to its nature. For the Hunter this is succeeding at a task which is important to you.

All the Triumph cards mean success in some way, but the Ace of Hearts is particularly strong. For example, the Queen of Hearts is called "Lady's Triumph" and means receiving extreme good luck, although that's not the same as the situation coming to an end. This Ace in particular tells of good endings. For a Hunter to Triumph the chase must be finished and the prize entirely in their hands. Hunter's Triumph means the bull's-eye has been hit, the trophy taken home, and you have gained the thing that you worked for.

Promise cards have a rising energy, Gambit cards resemble a sharp peak at the top which can fall to either side, and Folly cards a fall. By contrast, the energy of a Triumph is a stable, level line which stays at the maximum amount. All the up-and-down movement has finished and the situation is locked in to a full victory.

Triumphs often mean "Success!... of this flavor" or "Success!... if you do this." The Hunter's Triumph means getting your heart's desire, or at least the one you planned for, made an effort for, and earned. The story for this card features a silver arrow, famously a prize won by Robin Hood in the medieval ballads (in other versions, it's a golden arrow). This particular Triumph is also frequently linked to gaining an object or passing an important test, not just to emotion. If the reading covers an action, then the advice is to recognise what is most important to you in the situation and hold onto it. Make sure that the prize you are choosing is the one that you really want, no matter what anyone else thinks.

This is still a card about doing things alone and doesn't imply sharing or leaning on others. The Hunter's goal is often a measurable solo achievement instead of progress in a relationship. The happiness this Ace brings is strong, with a feeling of "Got it!" and the situation resolved in a way that makes you smile.

THE TWOS: THE LOVER

The number two in playing card divination traditionally refers to dealings between exactly two people. Not a crowd, not wider society, but love or business partnerships where another individual is the focus.

The Lover as a Role teaches us to connect fully to another person. It has moved from the solitary nature of the Hunter to including another in our world, letting them in past our normal barriers. There is an emotional bond with that person; they are not a stranger. The relationship itself could be personal or business but it connects the two of you directly. This Role doesn't look at how you interact with the wider population yet, only with this one other.

Such two-part bonds can be intense in comparison to the rest of the deck. The focus will nearly always be on the relationship, what you owe to the other partner, or potential risks of letting someone in. That risk can be love, friendship, financial, or something else, but when we see a Lover card appear, it will always direct us to look at who exactly it could be about.

With this Role the Magician's Journey takes its first step away from solo independence. It is a step that requires trust in another person, loving ourselves enough to be able to love others, and the bravery not to run from commitment. The Lover cards are about contracts and agreements between people. Even with our families and those we love most, there is a mutual agreement to do our best not to cause harm while making ourselves vulnerable to the possibility anyway. Holding up our own end of that deal requires more emotional stability than we might expect: we have to know what we want, respect ourselves enough to know where to put boundaries, and walk away if the trust is broken. We have to act selflessly for others, give love, and be part of something bigger. None of this is easy, but it is crucial to being more present in the world.

TWO OF CLUBS:
LOVER'S PROMISE
"AISLING WALKS IN AUTUMN LEAVES"

Hope, Romance and Fantasy, Comfort

Aisling could feel Orlaith there with her. She didn't doubt, not for a moment. They had walked together under these trees many weeks earlier, when the leaves were not as deep orange or brown as they are now and had not yet formed a carpet around their feet.

When they strolled along this path at the side of the castle, before Orlaith went to sea, her lover had given Aisling a green nut from a tree—and with it, a vow.

"When this nut dries and opens, I shall return to you. Keep it close and look for my ship on the horizon."

Aisling smiled to herself as she traced the same journey again, this time surrounded by the warm colours of the changed season. It was hard to be alone, but she held easily to the hope and trust they had for each other. When she thought of Orlaith, her heart knew that this was the anchor that made her world make sense, and that all the winds of winter could not trouble her if they were together. As she walked the same steps she had taken then, green grass now carpeted with fallen leaves, she studied the nut once more. It was opened and ready to share its goodness.

Aisling came to the end of the path in the gardens and to the high hill overlooking the docks. She gazed upon the calm sea and there, in the distance, saw the sails of a ship returning home.

Lover's Promise represents both hope and romance. It is a dream of wishes and potential, of the words we use to create a better future for someone. Like all Promise cards, it deals with beginnings and intends to create something substantial later, but until that comes along the message is to put aside cynicism and instead believe that good things can happen.

There is nothing wrong with the promises Lovers make to each other in the early days. They are sincere and meant truthfully. If your question was about another person, Lover's Promise shows somebody who will give you loyal support in times of need. It is the ideal of a new connection with someone who wants only good things for us.

The connection doesn't have to be romantic. The Lover as a Role overall gives and takes easily, forming bonds with a partner that range from purely emotional to more formal agreements such as business contracts. However, if it is a business-related matter, this will not just be a cold arrangement. It will be one which you believe in and which captures your needs.

Overall, this is a card of optimism and comfort. When you see it in a reading, the Promise is from someone you can trust. This trust—whether of a person or events—is an important part of allowing yourself to hope. We all have times when it feels difficult to hope and we're too tired or cynical to feel positive about how things will turn out. This card reminds us that the good and reliable must return. The card is saying, "It will be alright, let down your defenses, there is no danger here."

Lover's Promise also reminds us to take some time to enjoy ourselves, indulge fantasies, and see the beauty in the world. We should allow ourselves to believe the best about others and make grand plans without dismissing them as unrealistic.

TWO OF DIAMONDS:
LOVER'S GAMBIT
"LELA STEALS A KISS"

Emotional Risk, Agreements, Contracts

Lela ran breathlessly into the shadowed courtyard, straight into the loving arms of Vincenzo.

"What are you doing here? It's too dangerous!"

The taller figure had a more confident stance, and answered with a smile. "I had to see you."

Clutching him tightly, the young woman hurriedly checked the darkened space around them, but there was no one with a view of their hiding place. She protested again. "Our families would be furious! So close to the merger, with all Mother's money at risk. We—"

But her words were cut short as he kissed her roughly, and she quickly lost herself in returning it.

The night covered them almost completely, only made pale in places by a weak moon. The shifting shadows gave them time alone, but how long would it last? Lela felt a touch of excitement at the danger, but also a warm rush of love. As she turned her head, a fine chain earring with two red gems trailed down her exposed neck and glinted darkly under the moon's muted gaze. The night hid their secret.

This gamble was worth it, she reasoned. Tomorrow's business was full of risk, but intense connections such as theirs should not be denied.

Although this Role is called the Lover, the Twos govern all kinds of interactions with another person, including friendships and business contracts. It is rarer to see this Gambit apply to a strictly business arrangement unless it is also a matter of trust or great importance to you. More often this card is about emotional risk and taking exciting chances.

All Gambit cards are about making things happen in the way the particular Role does best, and for the Lover this is an honest and intimate conversation between two people. When we are completely alone we are safe from emotional connections to others. That is how the Hunter moves around the world: free of entanglements or having to concentrate on anything but themselves. When we open that space to include another person it can be a scary decision! Eventually we must do it, because everyone relies on others as we make our way in life. That risk is the Gambit—the need to trust that the other person will fulfil their end of the agreement.

As anyone who has been through it knows, you can only get to the dizzying highs of love if you take risks to get there. At some point, you will need to tell the truth about your feelings in a way which could backfire and cost you. This is one of the hardest Gambit cards to proceed with, because of that fear. However, the rewards of a successful Gambit are large. This could be a "yes" to a romantic question, or money in return for working hard on a contract.

Emotional honesty between friends and lovers is something we can all be better at maintaining. The Two of Diamonds requires us to actually do it—to forge good connections, make new partnerships, or strengthen old ones. Make a contract and mean it. This brave action can lead to great riches.

TWO OF SPADES:
LOVER'S FOLLY
"RICKARD FLOATS DOWNSTREAM"

Heartbreak, Argument, Angry Words

Rickard didn't want this. They'd fought, sure, but that was no reason to ... oh well, regrets wouldn't achieve anything at this point.

The two small boats met in the middle of the river. He tried one more time.

"I'm sorry. I didn't mean—"

"No more words. As of today, our partnership is ended." The other man held up the wooden stick and ceremonially broke it, dropping both parts into the water.

There was nothing more to say. Anger had pushed them apart, and it would be some time before it could be mended. Rickard nodded his head in acceptance but silently vowed to heal what was between them when he could.

The two vessels moved apart slowly, one north and one south, headed to opposite shores.

Every divination system has a reading to signify heartbreak and loss, and Lover's Folly is the classic one in this deck. All the Two cards directly represent two people, but where the other suits bring them together, this is the card that shows them breaking apart. It may not be in a romantic sense, but the Two of Spades always indicates an argument, conflict, painful emotions, or the ending of a partnership.

Linked with something like the Role of the Smith, this could be entirely about business, but more often it is emotional or even romantic. The one thing that can't be escaped is that this means bad feelings and an argument.

So, what can we do about it? No one likes receiving a card that means trouble, but there are several ways to think about the outcome that can make it better. Firstly, an argument is a temporary thing. Time can allow us to go back and ask forgiveness, or to forgive. Also, "trouble" is not the same as "disaster." It is unpleasant, but not critical. This is therefore a card that indicates a difficult road ahead but not always a serious problem. As this card is numbered two, at least this means that the difficulty is only with one other person.

The Lover is not interested in the whole of society, only in the more intense bond formed with a single individual. That bond can grow stronger but must also be able to become weaker, which is natural and necessary. Sometimes the only thing to do is recognise when you cannot achieve anything in that moment, and hold the door open for a reconciliation later when it is possible. Arguments happen, but you are in control of your actions. One choice you have is to forgive.

Finally, Lover's Folly is the first card to show an important rule: Folly cards are not automatically negative. Sometimes an argument is both necessary and the right thing to do. If a reading says that the other person is wrong and will cause harm with their action, your arguing or angrily debating with them is a good thing. If this card is an action you should take then it is time to say something that could cause an argument...because the alternative is going along with a situation you know is wrong. In that case you should do the difficult thing and explain why you want the opposite decision.

TWO OF HEARTS:
LOVER'S TRIUMPH
"YELEN LOOKS TO THE STARS"

Love, Partners, Intimacy

Yelen lay back on the grass and held Bata's hand, gazing up at the constellations spread above them. The hillside was full of quiet couples who had arrived for the fireworks and celebration earlier, but now that the festival was over only the quiet nighttime sounds of nature could be heard.

The light above had taken countless years to reach the arrangement it gave today, years as the planets and stars circled past each other, the pattern of the Dragon in its Den giving way to the Mother's Web and then up to the Great Tree. Yelen saw the bright dot of the Evening Star (which was in fact only a planet reflecting the sun) and in a perfect line leading from it the pattern known as the Sailor's Lamp.

Now the time was right for a wedding tomorrow. It was the most auspicious alignment. Her parents believed that this meant the relationship would last as long as the stars did, but the young woman knew better. Bata was already the foundation of the world to her, and whatever happened in her life from this moment, it would not involve them being apart for longer than they had to be. Messages written in the night sky would not change that.

The cold silver stars blazed on above but Yelen could feel Bata's loving hand in hers, the hot blood communicating the beat of their hearts in time with each other.

In nearly every divination system, the Two of Hearts represents success in love. There is also usually at least one card in a deck that signifies physical love and intimacy. In Lenormand readings the Lily is supposedly about purity and virtue, while other decks might mask it as marriage or emotions, but really they're being polite—those cards are about sex.

Lover's Triumph includes this definition too, as it covers all the connections between two people. It can refer to other types of bonds, but the action it suggests most frequently is to open your heart to another.

The best way to interpret this card is to concentrate on the fact that this is a Triumph. The Lover has made a Promise, worked a Gambit, overcome their Folly, and now achieves a final win—the two people involved are now in alignment, and all goes according to their plan. The meaning could apply to non-romantic relationships between two people, but it's quite intense if it does.

The energy of any Triumph card can be thought of as a line at maximum output that never falls. Because this card is specifically the Lover's Triumph, the success is gained in the way the Lover would do it. The Lover Role doesn't look far beyond their own boundaries: they are willing to interact with one other person who is important to them, but they haven't yet opened up to view the whole of outside society in the way the next Role, the Healer does. If you see this Triumph in a reading this means that it is definitely only about the connection to one other person.

In love, friendship, or any intense connection to another, the indication is of a strong and lasting bond. If there was any uncertainty between them previously, that is now gone. Needs are aligned, usually because both people know each other so well.

To be able to make this connection with anyone also requires the person to do something else first—be able to love themselves. The person has to believe that they deserve to be one half of a partnership. This can be easy to forget, and sometimes others in our lives will convince us that it isn't true. Both hearts in this Triumph are strong and successful, not just one, so for their love to endure, both must feel that they are worthy of it.

Overall this is a card of strong friendships, deep love, or at the very least a successful partnership based on acceptance and real understanding. The two hearts on the card are open to emotion and full of joy.

THE THREES: THE HEALER

The Lover teaches us to love ourselves and also love the one person who fits us. The Healer turns this love into compassion for many others—including strangers and wider society—and works to help them without asking for a reward.

The Role of the Healer can be one of the hardest to follow and to receive in readings. If you are angry at someone, the answers here give you no excuse to feed that anger; instead they demand that you act as a Healer, which is not always easy to do. Caring for others and forgiving them (even when they don't behave well) can be hard.

The Healer teaches us that it is okay to be angry or emotional but never to be cruel. Our emotions are our own concern, but our actions to others must always be better than that. In this way it is both a very peaceful and good influence on readings, as well as sometimes a difficult standard to live up to!

The Magician's Journey takes this expansion from two to many and educates the person on what that means in their life. Compassion is not an optional idea for Magicians. It is a critical life skill for everyone. Nobody gains real power, self-respect or happiness without having compassion for others.

The other lessons of The Healer build from that beginning. If you have compassion, is it worth anything if you don't act on it? How far do you go, before it becomes exhausting? What happens if you bring this into your life? The Healer is a very important Role for helping us decide who we are and how we will reach out to others before any of the later Role decisions can be made.

THREE OF CLUBS:
HEALER'S PROMISE
"HANNA AND THE SOLDIER"

Moral Decisions, Compassion, Principles

The young boy woke up and looked straight at Hanna, but he was too weak to move in the mound of blankets she had used as an emergency bed.

"Who are you?"

The woman replied in a calm voice. "A healer. I found you in the woods with that blade in your chest, brought you here." She nodded at the curved dagger on the table, still stained with his blood. She knew it well, since Arik, the town guard, had carried it these past three years.

The boy's eyes flicked to it, then quickly away. He could see that he was in a hut at night, with only a few flickering candles around the one room. He turned back to her and tried to sound brave. "You could have left me there."

"Yes." She didn't add the words that followed in her mind, "…especially as your army was attacking my people."

"Could have killed me too. But you didn't."

"No."

They waited in silence for the boy to ask the obvious next question. After a pause, he did.

"Why not?"

Sighing, the Healer folded a parcel of leaves in her lap and tried to put it into words that he would understand. And to convince herself too, because she was only half sure that her actions had been the right ones.

"I did it because you are very young, and very scared, and there's still time for you to learn that there are more important things than looking brave in front of your friends. I've seen into your eyes. You're not like the others yet."

"My people hate yours!"

"Yes. But you don't. And you don't like the killing. That means you can still learn the real lessons—that helping people makes you more impressive than hurting them. You'd be dead now if not for me. I'm no warrior, but I'll bet you find my skills quite impressive in this moment."

He swallowed, and eventually nodded.

"And besides, I took an oath. I help everybody, as long as it doesn't directly cause more harm to do so. In a way, I don't have a choice."

The boy's eyes narrowed. He made to get up but collapsed again when his body refused. "What do you mean? Of course you get a choice!"

"No, I don't. I swore to help all strangers, whether they were people I liked or not. Whether it would benefit me or not.

Whether they carried different beliefs or called another town home. You were dying, so I helped you. That is past, and of no concern."

Something in Hanna's voice caught his attention as her tone changed, and he turned cautiously to lock his eyes with hers once more.

"All of that is unimportant, boy. Look not to the past, but the future. You have your life again, but only because it was given to you by an enemy. What will you do with it? Who is your enemy now, and who is your friend?"

The Role of the Healer deals with how we relate to society, but its lessons are intensely personal. A Healer is someone who has made a choice to help others. While the Hunter was concerned only with themselves and the Lover focused on one other person close to them, the Healer must decide how they are going to interact with the whole of outside society.

This card is about making moral decisions. You have a choice to make, and one option is to act to heal the situation. Compassion through the Healer is not only for someone you have met and decided deserves your friendship—it is the choice to extend kindness to everyone before you know them.

There is an important second meaning which is not external at all. Many of us agree instantly that other people deserve kindness and to be treated fairly, but then don't do the same for ourselves. We judge ourselves by higher standards and assume failure in exactly the ways we would reassure friends aren't fair to do.

Healer's Promise is a reminder to all of us to be better. When it comes up in a reading it means that we should look very closely at which aspects of the situation could be looked at as a moral choice. It doesn't mean that you will give or receive compassion soon (putting compassion into action is the next card, Healer's Gambit). This is more about attitudes and tells you to look around at the kind and unkind people in a situation. A Promise is a vow, something you plan to do long-term. Are we only agreeing to make an effort if we get something in return? Are we rushing to judge someone, or assuming the worst? Are the people around you acting with good intentions toward you?

This card is one of the most important steps on the Magician's Journey. Compassion is sometimes seen as a lesser concept in divination and magic, but that is very wrong. It is the light in the darkness which shows real character. Many magical groups train their members to have a mental will that cannot be broken, and to see dominance or power as most important while leaving out any guidance on being kind to others. Those groups tend to produce terrible magicians with all the weaknesses that we see in the Folly cards: fearfulness, anger, egotistical and conflict-seeking behavior, and a lack of inner peace. That is not a path to strength. This card is a reminder to the reader that there is always a better way.

Compassion is not optional—it is a critical step for all spiritual and magical development. It does not make you weak, less successful, less respected, or less determined. In fact, compassion for others is the only thing that can give you real strength.

Strength does not come from your ability to do violence. (The Warrior Role looks at this topic as well, but the Healer knows it from a different direction.) Hate can make you feel strong and temporarily distract you from your fears, but you cannot use it to actually *be* strong. Real leaders and elders, those who are in control of themselves and get recognised for their spiritual strength, all demonstrate compassion often. It is very obvious whether a stranger has it or not.

Healer's Promise is a beautiful thing: a card symbolizing selfless compassion. Someone who does this will be seen as a light of healing and goodness the same way that the card itself is whenever it appears. No matter what the situation, a message of "someone here is acting selflessly" is always going to be welcome. When Healer's Promise appears, look closely for a decision that needs to be made. Examine how the individual is interacting with all of society, and whether the situation could be improved by a deliberate effort to be kind.

THREE OF DIAMONDS:
HEALER'S GAMBIT
"ANGELIQUE RECEIVES A GIFT"

Gift, Good Deeds, Assistance

This was the most delicate part of the negotiations. Their two houses were respected, but everyone knew that Angelique's family had nowhere near the wealth or connections of Robert Tessier. The day would require delicate protocol.

Everything came down to how much one side owed the other. If Robert would sit with them, accept food and drink, then the onlookers would know that Angelique could at least speak of financial matters. But what if he wouldn't sit? What if he called on any of the hundreds of obligations which would require them to match his gesture or appear rude? Her House did not have enough money to compete that way, and these talks would instantly be over.

She was surprised when he arrived. The man was younger than she'd expected, with green eyes and long brown hair. He smiled politely and bowed exactly the correct amount while she ran through the required words to allow them all to proceed.

She had just reached the second part of praising his grandfather's achievements when Robert interrupted.

"Before we continue, I would like to present you with something."

And as her despair grew, she watched him reach into a bag and produce a parcel wrapped in fine paper.

This was a disaster! She had no similar gift to give in return, nor could she have afforded one even if it had been planned. Angelique felt her eyes sting as she realized that it was over.

He continued: "This is one of my family's better treasures, a statuette in gold and sapphires. I believe it has become known as 'The Running Horse.'"

Even worse. The item he was holding was a legend, something so expensive that it was worth more than the holdings of her entire House.

"…And it is a gift to you. There is no obligation in return for this action."

Several people in the room gasped. Angelique blinked, and had to check that she had heard him correctly. He had just said the formal words which relieved her from need to give anything in return—and everyone had heard it! More than that, with this item on her side in the negotiations, they were now evenly matched for the rest of the day. It changed everything!

"Sir, you did not have to do this."

He smiled, and she decided that it was a smile she could grow to like.

"I know. But I see before me a woman who wears all the weight of others' expectations upon her and doesn't flinch, who *stood up in front of the people here today knowing that it could end badly but was determined to help her family for the right reasons. I have … a lot of respect for people who have that kind of strength."*

They proceeded to sit, she in a different chair from the one she had planned, able to use the one opposite him instead of the third seat to the side, now as an equal. And when they had finished the long, intricate words required before the first drink, he was still smiling, and she matched his with her own.

Where Healer's Promise was about the concept of compassion for others, this card speaks about an action. The meaning of Healer's Gambit is "gift": it could be a physical gift, given for good reasons, or it could be someone's time and energy. A Healer assists people, and putting that into action always results in a gift of some kind from one person to another.

Compassionate deeds support others, so while drawing this card won't cause an actual parcel to arrive at your door it is still always a very positive result to receive. This is also a Gambit card, which converts the Promise of the Role into action. Here, it is not enough to wish that things were nice; Healer's Gambit requires the Healer to take action in the world. Gambit cards also have an element of chance and risk, which in this case means that the Healer must perform the action without expecting a reward. It's possible that they will have done it for no personal gain (or not an immediate financial one, at least). However, Healers will quickly realize that behaving like this pays for itself: a Healer's reputation with people improves, and they act more positively. You as the Healer will also feel better about yourself, as doing good things for other people is one of the most well-known ways to improve your own sense of self-worth and happiness. You might think that people who spend effort on others for no immediate reward are foolish or being taken advantage of, but the rewards do come back to them.

Sometimes Healer's Gambit appears in a reading where it's very hard to see how it could belong. In those circumstances it often means "the rest of this reading is actually good for you, even if it doesn't seem so." It can mean "This seems bad, but it's actually a lucky escape." Since it is about your interaction with society, if it's in a position which has to be negative then it can mean there is a risk that people will disapprove of you.

Most often this card is more straightforward, meaning simply that you will receive assistance. This could put you ahead while needing no effort on your part or be the advice you need to help you move past an obstacle. It is a positive and a welcome sight in a reading.

THREE OF SPADES:
HEALER'S FOLLY
"PETER'S POOR EXCUSES"

Exhaustion, Undeserved Guilt, Overwork

Peter emptied the jug of water over his head and slid down the wall until he was sitting on the stone floor with his legs sticking out into the room. The sun shone hot outside, with a few rays slanting in through the narrow window of the castle.

Kat stepped over him and looked down with a scowl. "When was the last time you slept?"

Peter waved the question away. "I had to look after the soldiers they brought in."

"Really, all of them on your own? The last I checked, Captain Rob had three other people to help with that."

"No, I ... I want to contribute."

The older woman's voice softened. "I know you do. But if you don't eat and sleep soon, that won't be up to you."

The exhausted man continued to protest. "Now it's Elizabeth. Her temperature is better, but I must be there when she wakes up."

Kat's tone turned firm. "Don't be a fool. Drink more water, and rest. You can't help her if you're passed out on the floor."

"I ... yes, alright." Eventually Peter agreed, mostly because he wasn't sure he could lift his arms anyway. *"Wake me in an hour."*

The move from looking at only one partner or close family to interacting with the whole of society is not without its dangers. Some people find socializing invigorating, and some prefer it in smaller amounts, but a party has to end for everybody eventually. The demands of others can lead to tiredness and exhaustion if you do not rest and take time for yourself.

There are two main meanings with this card. The first comes from Healer's Promise, which signifies compassion. If you feel compassion for the whole world, you can quickly reach a point where it becomes too much to contain. Taking other people's pain onto yourself is a noble thing to do but can be a heavy burden over time. Simply being surrounded by a lot of people and noise for too long can be difficult, and the society a Healer deals with is very large and very demanding.

The second meaning is of foolish choices. Not every situation requires you to stride into it like a hero and decide that you should get involved to change it. Sometimes this makes it worse. It is a Folly of the Healer that they automatically assume they should act, when in fact they should either be resting or realizing that they don't have enough information to make the right choices.

By opening ourselves up to others, being compassionate, and making connections, we also open ourselves emotionally. This is good—life is for living, and healthy emotions should be explored! But opening and giving can easily lead to burnout or exhaustion if we don't also care for ourselves. Everyone has a limit, and this card suggests that the situation will test our boundaries.

One of the hardest lessons for all of us to learn is that we cannot help those we love if they are not ready. Patients have to make the decision to change before a helpful action from someone else will matter. Very often Healers and compassionate individuals will keep trying to make a change for someone else and be exhausted when they are ignored. It's just not true that you can fix anything or anyone if you try hard enough, the other person has to be ready as well.

The card's theme of exhaustion also applies to the thankless emotional work you do for others. Some people assume that those around them will take the hurts or aggravations of the day onto themselves automatically so that they don't have to. Healer's Folly is a good time to check that you are not being taken advantage of in this way.

So, this card means several things: the task may be tiring. Do not feel guilty if you personally don't fix all the problems in the world. Don't assume this is your fight. You can't help others if you don't look after yourself. Keep your emotional shields up. Consider not getting involved, and look at whether you need to stop and take a break. Make sure that the emotional effort you're spending is being appreciated.

As with many of the Folly cards, this overall meaning is not entirely negative—it is a chance to rest and to look after your own well-being.

THREE OF HEARTS:
HEALER'S TRIUMPH
"HAZEL BROUGHT TO JUDGEMENT"

Gratitude, Recognition, Teamwork

"Come in, Sister."

Hazel paused outside the door, then slowly opened it and walked into the large room. To her shock, the chairs around its walls were full of people. She had imagined that the Mother of the Order wanted to see her alone, maybe over the matter of the spy who had recently been revealed in the temple. Instead everyone was here, and some were smiling at her.

"I don't understand."

The Mother stood formally in a ceremonial robe, weapons at her waist. She gestured for Hazel to walk to the area in front of the main table. A window to the side illuminated whoever was in that spot.

The Mother spoke: "I hear that you were approached by the Spy, who we shall not name, on the day of their capture?"

"I was."

"And that you were offered a very great sum to betray us, a sum which your family certainly have need of."

"That is true."

"But you did not take the Spy's offer, and instead reported them. Why?"

"It wouldn't have been right."

There was a murmur from the crowd, but all eyes remained on the Mother. The leader continued.

"The Spy was a master manipulator. Others in the order could not resist them. But you did. When I told people this story, none of them were surprised."

There was a pause, during which Hazel wondered if she was supposed to say something. Eventually the Mother continued.

"Those who rise to our highest rank do not do so from a single test on one day. The recognition comes from a property of their character that is constant and long-term. It is clear to everyone that the character of such a Sister is already worthy. It is simply who they are, and who they will be tomorrow. None in this room doubt that you have become that person."

Hazel couldn't believe what she was hearing, as the Mother said the final words.

"Kneel, and be knighted."

The Healer Role is about dealing with the whole of society, and a natural result of someone choosing to act well is that they will be recognised for their good deeds. The final card of the Role deals with that conclusion.

Of course, a Healer doesn't do their Role in order to get personal fame. A bigger prize is the end result of what compassion brings to the person who practices it: an internal change to be happier, stronger, and supported by many friends. The Hunter and even the Lover are very much about you, but the Healer looks at how you interact with many people. The answer is that a good Healer puts others first—at least enough to cooperate, or to create healing, which can defuse a difficult situation and bring peace to all.

The type of success that comes with this Triumph therefore suggests teamwork with multiple people, and a response from them which is happy and filled with gratitude. Recognition for good actions is a very important thing to give and receive. It helps us feel seen and valued, and it shows others that we don't take them for granted. That we see the effort they have taken and are grateful for it.

Life can be exhausting, and work can be ignored. Recognition of small acts, generosity, or even of the person that you are, can be a vital part of building relationships. Check to ensure that you are giving this feedback to other people who deserve it, as well as demanding it for yourself when it has been earned.

If this card appears in the reading in a way which suggests you need to take an action, then look for ways to involve others in teamwork. Make sure that you are giving respect to people properly and not assuming that they just know you are grateful.

Most of all, recognise that our actions can bring good or bad reactions from people and the only way to be sure that our connections to strangers are going to turn out well is to be a Healer and to make peace.

THE FOURS: THE SMITH

The Smith is a blacksmith, using skill to bring many elements together according to a plan, creating something new, and eventually collecting the reward for their hard work. In numerology and divination the number four is a calm and stable one, and this Role generally is as well. The Smith is also linked to the traditional associations of the element of Earth: many of their tools are heavy, solid, unyielding, and are linked to the home, work, and money.

The Smith can be any gender but is always a figure of calm stability. The four pips on the card can be seen as corners of a room, holding up the walls and giving a quiet space to work within.

In the Magician's Journey, the Smith represents the next step after the Healer. We have moved on from having a good relationship with outside society and now have to decide what we're going to build in that society. A Smith creates, has a career, makes long-term plans for earning, and in doing so produces items which support the whole community. The lessons the Role teaches are of patience (such a difficult task for many of us!), the need to keep learning new things, and using our time to create the kind of order we want. Most of all, it teaches that while work and physical items are important, they are not more important than people. A skill or career is fulfilling and provides good services to others, but objects are just objects. The Magician continues on afterward in the search of deeper meaning.

FOUR OF CLUBS:
SMITH'S PROMISE
"DINRI AND THE SHINING CITY"

Long-term Work, Planning, Patience

Two people sat lazily in comfortable chairs, sipping their wine. Carolyn liked the look of this little-known Dinri, with their rich clothes and quick eyes. She asked them about the coming elections.

"Tell me, who do you support, Marius or Ezade?"

"Of the two, I must support Ezade."

She raised an eyebrow at this. That choice was the younger one, known to be hasty and prone to big decisions. That didn't sound like Dinri at all.

"Wh—"

Before she could even finish, they spoke again in their odd, calm voice.

"Do you know of the City of Lapis? The treasure of the Eastern Isles, home to the four Wonders?"

"No, I've never heard of it."

"The gates to the city are made of black stone, rising up from the stormy sea to brace the high, strong walls. In the Merchant's Quarter, endless stores are filled with chests and carpets, showing

the glittering wares, as spices scent the air. In the Great Library, scholars from every land study all the works that can be found, sharing the wisdom they find across borders. And then there are the Gardens, stretching from the south wall to the central Spire many miles inland, each serenaded by the gentle murmur of sparkling fountains. The opera house! The forges and workshops, boat yard and observatory! Citizens can eat, be amazed, perform art, and work together as they wish."

Carolyn gazed at the mysterious figure, entranced. "And where can I find this city?"

Dinri shook their head. "It doesn't exist yet, and won't for another seventeen years."

She blinked, confused. "Seventeen? That's … very specific."

"Yes, that's why I need Ezade to win. She won't help directly, but next year is the election of the new Head of Building Projects. And only Ezade will pick Nalen. Nalen will definitely approve the plan I need for the shipment of gold and stone, meaning that in five years' time I'll be able to convince the Council to begin the Library."

Carolyn put her drink down, suddenly feeling distance from someone who could hold grand plans in their head with such intimidating clarity. Even as she desperately wanted to see the outcome of the project, she decided that it would be as an investor, not a romantic partner.

"Tell me more."

The Smith's Promise is a plan for long-term work that will bring a great reward when completed. It is the farmer looking at an empty field and seeing a full harvest in the future. It says that a thing can be done with low risk, although it will take steady work.

The Smith creates beautiful masterpieces but also all the mundane items we need to keep our homes secure and comfortable. They deal in the heavy tools and metals of the forge: hammer, anvil, fire, air, water, and earth. From this they produce objects essential for daily living.

Now, "this needs planning and could take a long time" is not a reading many people want to see! It's hardly as exciting as taking a risk with Lover's Gambit, or as immediately rewarding as Hunter's Triumph. But this card can still be a great result because the act of planning gives us a special way of thinking about something. A plan before any work has started can be about an ideal version, unspoiled by any need to compromise. Plans still have time to improve the end result since we aren't yet locked into a fixed schedule. In a way, a plan can be as perfect as a dream; the gift of time to keep improving is one we'd all like to receive.

If a timescale is needed in the reading then this card says that it is definitely not going to happen immediately, but also reassures us that the end result will eventually be worth it. This is an early promise of something that will end in a great reward. It also gives the path which will be required: the only route from here to the Triumph is to actually do all of the work, not to avoid it.

As with the other number fours, this card brings a sense of calm and stability to the reading. Nothing is going to happen right now and the conditions are right to start some good work. Even if we wanted the prize to come to us more quickly, that period of safety and predictable time can be a nice result. Have patience, and build something worthy of the time that will go into its creation.

FOUR OF DIAMONDS:
SMITH'S GAMBIT
"FIONA'S MASTERPIECE"

Creation, Skilled Work, Planned Change

Fiona stepped out of the smithy and took some deep breaths of the cold air. She looked at the land all around, changed once again by the seasons. Now it was covered in frost and ready for the snow, but when she had started living in this remote village the green shoots of spring had been everywhere. In that time, she had worked on everything she could to raise money: kettles, horseshoes, gate hinges, small nails. Tools for the farmer, the baker, the shepherd.

And every evening, when the work was done and her time was her own, she added to her masterpiece. Two iron gates, tall and delicately turned, full of arcs and intricate leaves shaped in metal. Shadows on the ridges were highlighted in silver. The gates were the key which would earn her entry to the Guild and to the title of Master.

No one in the city would have seen such as these, for she had poured all of her love and hopes into them, week after week in stolen moments and late-night freedom. Once she had the title, she could marry Dougal.

Next Spring my masterpiece will be ready, she thought, and smiled out at the frosted landscape surrounding the smithy.

Gambit cards involve a risk that may be won by using the skills of the Role. For the Smith, that must be about creating something new and the peril that it will either break completely or just not be of high enough quality. Creating anything can be intimidating—people might judge you on the results, or you may have only one opportunity to get it right. Don't let their opinions hold you back from making art. The Smith loves to create, is good at it, and will bring something new and valuable into existence.

In a reading, this card can cover a very wide range of options. The only rule is that the Smith's creation is never instinctual, only planned. They work from a template and know what they're going to do—you can only forge metal by learning the rules and sticking to the process, the right temperatures and techniques in the right order. This means that if the item does fail, it is mostly due to the Smith's skill. Chance and chaos are only small factors here.

If you were to apply Smith's Gambit to a romantic situation, it could mean moving on to a new stage of building a life together such as marriage. It could easily mean starting a family, but only if it's planned! (Several readers were shocked to see this card appear in romantic readings, and are reassured when it's explained that this won't mean a surprise!)

In its widest definition, Smith's Gambit means "something which wasn't here before." The situation the cards are revealing will have a new element introduced, as part of a deliberate decision. If the rest of the reading is highly chaotic then the Smith brings a measure of order—this creation takes time and there are choices to be made in that time which will definitely affect the end result. Many other Gambit cards (the Diamonds) deal with risk or the unknown. The steady, calm nature of the Four of Diamonds brings more predictability to this one, along with the twinkling potential for profit. You can always succeed or fail in a task, but the Smith has tools and knowledge to make sure that the journey towards their Triumph is more dependable than most.

FOUR OF SPADES:
SMITH'S FOLLY
"NELL CLINGS TO THE WINDOW"

Greed, Inertia, Obsession

The Skull of Rathek! A large cobra's head made of purest gold, with shining red ruby eyes and sharp extended fangs! A work of such beauty and wealth that generations of treasure-seekers had fought to own it. Rumored to have been found in a hidden desert temple, every woman and man who claimed to possess it had died soon afterwards, leading to the belief that the item was cursed. Still the glowing golden tones of its menacing curves capture the greed and imagination of more victims.

The latest two are climbing the outside of the mansion where it currently sits on display. Reaching the top floor window, they peer into a room that is more like a vault. Deep brown wooden panels line the walls and luxurious carpets adorn the floor, but these are simply traps for the unknowing thief. Beneath the flooring are weighted levers ready to sound alarms. In the walls there are lethal crossbows waiting to fire. And if one were to touch the table itself where the skull sits invitingly on a red velvet cushion, well …

"It can't be done, Joe! You know what the old man said—if you step on the carpets, the guards'll come and grab you!"

"So we'd need to jump from there, by the door, over the whole rug and onto the raised bit with the table on it, in one big leap."

"Let's go back. This isn't worth it. We'll never get away with the stupid thing. We could have been making proper coin at the festival, but all you've talked about for weeks is this room, drawing maps, reading the old man's books..."

But Joe had that look in his eyes again, the one which said that he wasn't listening or seeing anything except the candlelight flashing from the scales of the golden snake head on the table. "Enough, Nell! I'm going in."

Through the window was easy, and onto the safe area of floor beneath it, but then he had to prepare. Flexing his legs, Joe sprang—and landed just beyond the carpet, wobbling to keep his balance!

Nell followed him in, and made the same jump—successfully, although she landed farther to the left and couldn't reach him. Joe ran ahead to the small raised platform which held the table. He knew not to step on the paler wood at the top, as crossbows were waiting to fire on anyone who did that. Avoiding the traps, he finally approached the table itself.

"Please, Joe! Come away. It can't be that easy!" She whispered urgently, reaching for his arm.

"I told you, Nell! We can have it! Look at its eyes, those are rubies, real rubies..."

He put his hand out for the skull just as Nell pulled his shirt hard enough to yank him backward ... and it was well that she did, for at that moment needles shot up from the table, glistening with poison! Joe fell against her in surprise, the two of them hitting the top step ... and crossbow bolts flew through the air right above their heads as they lay low on the floor. A loud bell started to clang, and Nell pulled Joe again, this time back to the window and out into the night. They cleared the opening just as the heavy door to the room crashed open revealing armed guards. Despite the danger, Joe couldn't stop looking back to the treasure on its cushion, the sharp fangs promising adventure and riches ... but not today. Fleeing the grounds by Nell's side, he muttered to himself:

"I nearly had it. It was nearly mine!"

The Smith's Folly is most simply described as greed, but a more subtle description could be "thinking that objects are more important than people." An artisan can become obsessed with a project, working long hours and putting it before their health or relationships. While the Role of the Smith deals with orderly work and skill, it's also important to keep your eye on the real goal. The point of a long-term project is still to create something, not just to endlessly do work. The useful tools or beautiful objects created should benefit people and bring something to the world. Even if the goal is only to earn money, look again at what use that money is eventually put toward—*that* is what really matters, not the hours of work.

There is more to life than working. If you are very lucky, your career can also be fulfilling and enjoyable, but take care to balance it with the other essential components of a happy life. This Folly indicates that you may not be seeing things clearly and are in danger of ignoring the good advice from those who are close to you.

The other meanings of Smith's Folly are inertia and perfectionism. The Smith hopes to create something, work on it, and then be paid when it is ready, but nothing gets done if you lose yourself in the work. The number four has many associations with a slow and stable pace that can be taken to extremes (especially when what you want is speed). If you're asking about the timing of an event, this card indicates delays due to being busy doing something else.

Smith's Folly can even refer to hoarding of wealth, or rampant greed. In all cases, it comes from wrongly thinking that possessions, wealth, and status symbols are important in themselves, or that everything you create must be perfect no matter how long that takes. Items can have value in providing security or comfort for you to live your life, but they are just objects and should never come before people.

This card's perfectionism aspect might be the biggest problem. Many people these days believe that they (and any work that they are judged by) must be perfect every time. This is impossible, and no way to live. None of us are making their final masterpiece today or competing for the gold medal at an Olympics. Instead, we are in training, all of us, to gain experience and be a little better tomorrow. This requires us to fail. Failing is the only way for us to learn anything and is very normal in the act of creation. Try something, fail at it. Try it again. Get a bit better. Try it ten times more. It's better still. Keep failing.

The fear of failing even once is what makes people seek perfection and what stops the Smith from finishing their work. If they can keep adjusting it some more, it will be closer to perfect … but never actually released into the world. This card says that we should stop aiming for the absolute best every day and allow small imperfections. Anything else leads to so much inertia that we'll never reach the goal. Alternatively, like Joe in the story, we'll aim only for the Gold Medal as a first step and take too many risks to try to bypass the steady work and repeated failures that the Smith must go through to be successful.

Look carefully at your priorities when this card is drawn. It is a warning to make sure that you are not doing any of the negative actions above. Focus instead on balancing the work and results with people and relationships in your life, instead of going too fast, too slow, or dismissing everything for a shiny but unrealistic prize.

FOUR OF HEARTS:
SMITH'S TRIUMPH
"OLD FU EATS A PEAR"

Harvest, Order, Fairness

Old Fu sat on the bench next to the basket of fruit. He reached in and picked up a large, ripe pear, breathing in its scent. Closing his eyes, he concentrated on the important business of appreciating the fresh smell.

A young woman beside him looked at the basket curiously and asked her question again. "Please, what helped you the most in becoming the Master of your school?"

He took a delicate bite from the juicy pear, thinking over his words.

"Before I learned fighting, I was a farmer. That is what made me great."

They sat in silence for a moment, until she realized he wasn't going to explain further. She tried again.

"But how did that make you into a fighter?"

Looking out over the field where children were playing, Fu responded:

"When you are a farmer, you must be aware of everything around you. The ground, the weather, the animals that might eat

your crops. You must know when the right time to harvest comes, when the storms will strike. An artist can sit down and start painting at any time, but a farmer has to wait for the seasons. You must learn to find the best time and use it. That is why I was superior to others in a duel—they thought they could start fresh at any time, but I was content to wait and read the signs. Farming taught me patience. It taught me that hard work pays off, even if the reward is a year from now. And it taught me to take opportunities when outside forces converge in the right way, to see the openings and use them."

Old Fu's mastery had ensured that the school prospered over the years and supported the growing family around it. He bit into the pear again, seeing in his mind the full fields of wheat, trees heavy with fruit. Yes, he thought, after the harvest when the crop is safely in and you have earned its bounty through honest work … that is the sweetest time of all.

Smith's Triumph is a reward that arrives after a period of deliberate work. It's a finished sword blade after a long night of hammering in the forge, or a collected harvest brought in and on its way to market.

Unlike Smith's Promise, which says there will be a reward in the future, the Triumph symbolizes something coming to you now due to past efforts. It is safe, but above all it is fair. While other Roles look at good luck or big successes, this one is calmer: it may not be spectacular, but you will receive what you worked for. Certainty can often be a lot more useful than flashy chances.

This reward will not be as personally important as the Triumph for the Role of the Hunter, but it also doesn't require the Hunter's absolute commitment. The Smith's work is more conventional and predictable with an end product that pays the bills.

When you see this card in a reading, it means that a long-term prize will be yours, one that has been earned and is deserved. The "prize" is rarely a single item or money—instead, it's often a reaction to a long-term situation. More than once it has shown people coming together to help a friend who has been there for them reliably in the past and can now be supported in turn. The Smith's energy is stable and slow, but the results are visible to all and appreciated. This is an earned success.

THE FIVES: THE WARRIOR

The Warrior's number is five, because (unlike the balanced and stable four of the Smith) the Warrior exists to take action. They are not a patient guard but a wandering sword who is only defined by their skills. Action is the way in which they gain fame and approval, but it is also a philosophy: warriors believe it is right to take action, that we should make changes in the world which cannot be undone, and that we should force progress to happen through our efforts.

The four previous Roles have been less disruptive. They involved working out who you are, who to let in, how to get along in society, and what is created for the self when left alone to do so. The Warrior is very different—this Role has decided to go out into the world and kick over some furniture. They are going to bring change to the way things are, because they want that change to happen even if others don't.

The Warrior's active mentality can be very positive. After all, there are good reasons for seeking change, in others and in ourselves, but the Warrior takes on a lot of responsibility when they make that choice. Dealing with that responsibility is a large part of this Role, and it is also the main lesson in the Magician's Journey at this point.

The Warrior has some of the most important and difficult lessons of any Role, ones we all come back to. Being a Warrior requires us to confront our fears, choose issues we will take a stand for, control ourselves even when we're passionate about a cause, and speak even when society tells us to be quiet. All of these things are incredibly difficult. Fear on its own can prevent us from taking action or make us look for excuses, while emotion turns easily to anger. Not all the consequences can be known before the decision has to be made.

Mastering this Role gives the Magician the decisiveness and control to make positive change.

FIVE OF CLUBS:
WARRIOR'S PROMISE
"TEMIR OF THE THREE CHIEFS"

Conflict, Necessary Opposition, Resistance

The swords clashed again as the two muscled warriors threw themselves into the fight. From the sidelines, three elders of the tribe kept an experienced eye on the duel.

The one on the left spoke first. "What do you think of the merchant and his latest threats?"

The others considered this for a moment. On the right, Chagatai made a noise of disgust while continuing to watch the training match. "I told you at the start of the year. We need to fight these people. Their 'concerns' are always the same and end up with them in power and the innocent trampled underfoot. What of you, Temir? I suppose you will counsel peace, as always?"

There was another pause, and the middle figure spoke.

"No. Not this time."

To the surprise of the others, more words followed. "The tribe to the East have been our neighbors since my grandmother's days. Now this merchant and his army have come in, trying to turn us against our friends. They say that people from other places are lesser. They say that the poorest in our halls are a threat to us.

They say that our friends who have children among our village should be sent away. They poison the minds of the young and would ruin our reputation with the other lands."

The two elders were amazed, for they hadn't heard Temir say more than a single word in judgement for many years. Gesturing to the fighters in front of them, he continued.

"Here are two boys who grew up together. In all my rulings where peace talks between enemies can heal a divide, I counsel that way. I do this because I want our people to live to be old. But this enemy today will not respect peace. His power is from hate, and he intends to use the hate he can stir in the people to gain only more power. He would turn one boy against his friend. You cannot fight that poison with words. You cannot allow the village to think it is something worthy of debate. It is not. It is not part of any real discussion, only an evil man's lies."

The three of them considered the young fighters again, as one of the youths strained against the other's shield.

"I hope these boys will live to be old. But there is no way that we can allow the merchant to spread his story in our village and remain the people we are. In many disputes, I counsel peace. But this poison … this we fight."

If you have a cause you believe in, it means that you want to change things from the way they are now. The current situation isn't good enough, and you want to improve it. There are valid reasons for being a warrior in today's society, but you must accept that taking action to increase your cause will reduce someone else's. Any change you make in the world will affect everyone it touches. For the Warrior Role, this action is needed, so they accept that conflict will be the result.

This Role is not about an argument between people like the Two of Spades. It is a bigger decision, to *oppose*. Nearly every situation covered by the Warrior Role does not actually mean violence, but primarily action, and conflict.

A funny thing happens when someone trains to be a warrior. You see it most often in martial arts or sports that include fighting. When someone feels confident that they can protect themselves, they fear strangers less and they become less aggressive. People who train to fight will often become calmer and choose nonviolent solutions whenever they can, simply because they are less afraid. This is the flipside to the conflict this card signals: it doesn't have to happen. The Warrior's Promise means "Conflict," but it can be a sign to take steps now to avoid that conflict in the future … and that choosing to do so is a very good idea. The Warrior who stands ready to protect others but never has to take their weapon out of its scabbard is one who never runs the risk of attacking when they shouldn't. Restraint is an excellent antidote to conflict.

However, sometimes conflict is both necessary and the right thing to do—either to protect others, or to fight for your beliefs. You must look very carefully indeed to see that you are not leaping in when you could have chosen a peaceful solution, but also that you are not neglecting your duty to protect the vulnerable. Conflict has consequences, and you should always think carefully before engaging in it. That does not mean it is never the right answer; sometimes it is necessary.

It's important not to take this card as justification for acting on hate. There is a *very* big difference between being motivated to act because you are angry at injustice and being driven by hate. Disagreeing with the way things are because you can see that they are unfair or wrong is valuable: as long as it prompts you to fight for a better world for everyone, it is not a bad thing to feel. Anger can be extremely good at motivating people to make real changes in social equality and justice.

Hate, on the other hand, never works. Hate for another is not acceptable, nor is it helpful to you. It always ends badly (a theme the Warrior's Folly looks at in more detail).

When this card appears in a reading, remind yourself that some battles are worth fighting—but also look very carefully at whether you are doing the right thing.

FIVE OF DIAMONDS:
WARRIOR'S GAMBIT
"ELENA ON THE BURNING SANDS"

Courage, Overcoming Fear, Taking Action

Elena clutched the weapon in her hands and tried not to tremble. It felt reassuringly heavy and would be good enough for the job today. The sands of the arena were hot under her feet, the sun blinding.

She thought back to her training with Mertis.

"When the time comes, you will feel fear. That is normal."

"Demitrius doesn't seem to fear. He stands like a mountain."

"That is an act for appearances. Every living thing feels the rush in their body when a dangerous situation begins. It is good, it keeps you alive. Feeling fear is never a cause for shame or concern. When it happens, simply know that the event has begun and you are ready to take action."

Elena adjusted her grip on the sword and held her breath. She hated the way that fear made her want to hide, to give in. The emotions churning in her stomach took on a hard edge, and she briefly used the burn of anger to replace them. Then she allowed it to drain away, remembering Mertis's guidance on that as well.

"Anger is not your friend. If you have been wronged, it can give you motivation. But if anger is demanding to be felt because you do not like to be afraid, ignore it. You are a warrior, one who must never lose themselves to mindless rage. Your responsibility is too great. The weapon in your hand must only go where you choose, never where anger would throw it hastily. When one warrior is calculated and the other is angry, it is the first who will stand at the end of the day."

"But my feet don't want to move. How do I begin when it is so important that I must not fail?"

"For some, being the silent mouse until the predator has passed overhead is an option. It is not so for a warrior. Others rely on your actions to protect them. The only route you have through fear is to take action to resolve the threat. If you want to feel less fear, use your blade to slice pieces from your enemy until they are smaller."

Elena grinned at the memory. Mertis was one of the kindest people she knew, and her words had been a joke, but they were still true in a way. Her training had slowly allowed her to recognise her fear as a signal to act. It had been hard, but her ability to acknowledge the fear without being overwhelmed by it had grown ... until today.

Her opponent stepped out onto the sands. The two were to be judged on their skill, and the ability to fight without injuring the other. Still, accidents could happen, and the danger was real. Her stomach wasn't feeling any better, but that discomfort was *the background noise of the warrior's life. Taking a breath, she stepped forward.*

When we talk about Courage, what we're really talking about is fear. It's a good topic, because fear affects all of us on a daily basis and is the motivation for a vast range of human behavior. When we try to get down to the real cause of many of the negative things we do, the answer is simply fear.

An issue many people face every day is the fear of failure. We're told all the time that failure is bad, that there are winners and losers and you don't want to be a loser. However, this isn't how the world works at all. Failure is the only way we learn anything (quite literally: the brain finds it harder to remember things if we get them right the first time). Successful people are nearly always those who fail, and fail, and fail, and then succeed after a lot of practice. Perseverance is much more important than skill.

A fear of failure means that a lot of us don't take action. The Smith's Folly previously signified perfectionism where we don't want to release a project because we're afraid it's not good enough yet (or we rush for the top prize because we don't want to fail even once). The Warrior's fear starts earlier, at the very beginning of an action. We procrastinate or find excuses not to start. We put up walls against others and stay in bad situations because it's scarier to take a risk on something new. We hesitate and worry over situations where we don't want to fail. In short, fear is the reason that most of us don't go out and make big changes in the world today. The Warrior is a Role which is determined to take action and fear is the biggest block to that happening.

This card is one of courage, specifically the type that overcomes freezing out of fear and allows us to proceed into action. The first step to following this is not to be ashamed or afraid of feeling the fear itself. It is a natural emotion, and a healthy way of your brain telling you to be careful. True courage does not require you to never feel fear at all, it is feeling it and being determined enough not to let it stop you carrying out the action anyway.

If the Warrior is to fulfil their Role and act decisively, making change that affects others, they absolutely have to confront fear. As well as preventing new beginnings, fear also makes people aggressive and angry. The plan is that by aggressively driving away the thing causing the fear, the warrior will stop it happening again. In this way, fearful people support violence and oppression in order to feel safer. Look very carefully at your emotions and actions if you find yourself thinking along those lines. You do need courage, but overcoming your fears must not change the good intent of the action you had planned.

Courage never means "feel fear, ignore it, and blindly charge ahead without thinking about it." True courage comes from not letting fear turn your good intentions into bad results. The subject of the reading must overcome personal challenges and be able to act instead of being stopped, but they must also keep the quality of that act as pure and beneficial for others as it was when they planned it.

The Warrior's Gambit is to step onto the battlefield and take a stand for what they believe in. All Gambit cards signify action, but this one may be the most physical and high energy in the whole deck. Courage is loud, and the effects of a worthwhile act will be felt strongly by other people. When this card is seen the person should look at the fears which are holding them back from supporting a worthy cause and courageously defeat them.

FIVE OF SPADES:
WARRIOR'S FOLLY
"FERGHUS, SHUNNED AND ALONE"

Acting Rashly, Dishonourable Actions, Shame

Ferghus sat upon the stone floor, listening to the chatter of the people outside. All was lost. So many years of dreaming that they would one day chant his name, call him a hero, and now ... that was gone forever.

It had taken only a few seconds. A burst of anger, and a thrust of his spear against a kinsman who had no defense. The people hail you and thrill to see your prowess when you have honor, but one mistake can take it all away. No one follows a brute who attacks the weak, no one praises an unfair fight caused by rage.

He saw the way they looked at him as he walked through town. They were afraid. His muscles were a threat now, and in place of a hero they only saw a dangerous animal who couldn't be trusted to restrain himself.

All gone. The respect, the glory ... he would never gain a new name in song to replace this, his tale would always include the angry actions of the past day no matter what else he accomplished in the future.

The warrior picked up his spear and studied the intricately engraved handle, lost in thought again. Then he threw it to the floor in disgust.

The Warrior makes change happen. They act, and other people have no choice about being affected by those actions. This puts a heavy responsibility on the Warrior to be sure that their reasons are the best ones, every time.

It is not easy to be a Warrior in today's society. Opposing others will always cause some to hate you or be afraid of you. You have one chance, only one ever, to stay on the narrow road where your actions are justified and necessary. If you mess that up, you are done—you become someone who must be kept away from others for the safety of all.

Warrior's Folly concentrates on our Reputation, and how delicate it is. This isn't the same as fame or how well-known we are, it is how much honor and respect we have managed to keep. Most of us don't think we've done anything worthy of respect (we don't leap into a burning building to save people or discover medical cures) but that's not where the line is. The relevant questions are: "Can you be trusted by others? Do you make the right choices?"

This choice might be to keep going to school or work every day, instead of not going. As the Smith knows, long-term work is a hard decision that takes effort. They keep making the effort daily to provide for those they love, instead of robbing a bank or leaving town to live on a beach.

The danger of reputation for the Warrior is not that you didn't do enough, it's that you did the wrong thing just once. Anger is an emotion we all feel, but very few of us can deal with it well. We either let it spill out and affect people or turn it inward and damage ourselves. The only way to deal effectively with anger is to let it go. Acknowledge that it exists and don't be frightened by that. Look at why it exists, what your body and mind are telling you to be afraid of or to confront, but then move on to the next stage without the loss of control that anger can bring.

The Warrior has to be aware of anger because conflicts that inspire us to make change often cause us to feel anger as well, about the unjust or unfair nature of current reality. If we didn't care, we wouldn't be driven to change things. A lot of issues in modern life seem simple, but one mistake that will always ruin a warrior's reputation regardless of what they are trying to do is to act in anger. They must be more honorable than that.

Warrior's Folly appearing in a reading is primarily a warning not to rush into action. It's a card about moving too fast and making bad decisions from rage or pride. This can lead to shame (as well as rejection by society). This does not mean that such an outcome will definitely happen, it is only a warning that it could—steps can still be taken to protect against it. Seeing this card therefore sends a message that says "Danger! You could mess this up. Check really carefully that your motives are right, and that your actions won't affect others in a bad way. Put insurance against that into place now, not later. And don't rush!"

Honor is not separate from your life, even if you think that parts of the Warrior Role couldn't apply to you—there is no division of your health, work, family, home, and then somewhere over in the corner, honor, which is something vague to do with knights fighting each other. Honor is your whole life; it is how you spend every second of your day. This doesn't mean you have to follow some kind of military code—you can be anyone and spend your time doing anything. It simply means that when you make a decision, you ask the following questions: "Do I care if I harm others?" and "Am I willing to take actions that put 'not harming others' ahead of me getting the maximum that I can?"

This card means that the situation contains the potential for the person to mess up in such a way that they will appear shameful or dishonorable. They need to look carefully at how they are communicating with people and whether their motivations are the right ones. They should tread carefully and make sure they are beyond reproach.

FIVE OF HEARTS:
WARRIOR'S TRIUMPH
"AMBASSADOR LEVAN'S GAME"

Victory, Beating Stronger Opponents, Safety

"Do you play chess, Ambassador Levan?"

"I am aware of it, but we have a different national game our-selves." The ambassador sat comfortably in robes, in contrast to the visiting general's stiff military uniform. *"We do not like chess very much."*

The general spluttered slightly, so Levan explained. *"Chess only deals with domination and destruction. It starts with equal armies and allows equal turns. When you have moved, your opponent always has the chance to move. The only interactions are in terms of military might—the Knight never gets to ask the Pawn about her childhood. Our cultural game, named Drannet, is very different."*

He brought the general to a large table at the side of the room that hosted a Drannet board. The enemy clearly did not know what he was looking at, so after a moment Levan was forced to point to the pieces. *"This is our board game."*

"This? But ... there are trees on it! It's not even flat. I thought this was a map of the region. How do you even play on that?"

"It can be difficult to see if you are used to chess. We start at opposite ends of the board, here ... and here. There are many ways to play. Our forces may be armies, or townsfolk, or animals seeking shelter. We may cooperate, or not. We grow our population and expand at our own speed. There is a lot of randomness: we use small glass beads to represent the elements and weather, and drop them directly onto the board. Water falling on a forest has a very different effect to fire upon a village."

The general had no reply, staring at the landscape laid out before him. Rivers and streams cut through dark woodland, across green fields. Mountains rose to one side and a village could be seen at the other end.

"On this particular board," Levan continued, "it is full summer. In our hemisphere that means the sun is at the height of its power. The rules therefore change, and the sun influences play. It banishes darkness, removes all the shadows which could be used to hide secrets. It exposes lies and allows only for the energetic pursuit of truth. In the spirit of that, I will speak truth to you now: we desire peace with your nation."

The general agreed to peace, which Levan had expected. It was easily said, although the other culture was so warlike that he doubted their words would last longer than it took them to prepare to invade. However, the ambassador had kept the situation of seasons on the board deliberately simple for the newcomer. In reality, the time was a little past summer and the moon was almost an eighth returned. This allowed for a small concealment *of the plan, one which was not entirely made of straight lines and truth.*

From the corner of his eye, Levan saw the guards of both nations stationed at the door begin to talk to each other. Curious already, flirting a little. He smiled. This was one route to peace. These visitors saw everything in terms of dominance, owning resources, demonstrations of strength, but life wasn't like that. Soon there would be families between their peoples—and who were they going to heed when a government told them they must now fight each other? In so many other subtle ways, Levan had spent the past few months preparing the borders and the people so that the enemy would find it quite impossible to launch an attack. Victory was already his, and this visiting general didn't even know which game had been played.

"Now, let us move on to your military parade, General. I understand your soldiers look very fine." Levan shook his head at the flags and troops lined up outside that were supposed to mean something. Chess players, ugh.

Unlike most of the other Roles, the Warrior takes up opposition to something or someone. Victory therefore refers to victory over an opponent. This being a Triumph, it also means a clean and lasting victory, one with no doubt around it.

There are several things the Warrior wants to do: by taking action, they have already beaten procrastination and fear, which can be a victory in itself. This success is even bigger than a brave beginning because it is reached while someone actively opposes you and it brings a definite end to the threat, and new safety afterwards.

A Triumph was originally a Roman parade, to praise a commander who was successful in war. In the Warrior's Triumph, this means that you will not only win but will be seen to win by others. All of this means that when the card is shown in a reading it symbolizes a decisive, total victory with safety after it. The conflict can involve anger or disagreement, but it will be settled. The kind of causes that we choose to oppose in modern life can be much bigger than ourselves and there are forces in politics or society which can seem impossible to beat. This Triumph is the one which is strong enough to do so. Alternatively, the opponent might be ourselves. Some of the hardest habits and beliefs to defeat are our own, the ones we believe too difficult to change.

This Triumph describes a turning point, after which everything is gloriously better. It can be successful resistance to a larger force, or overcoming something difficult in your own mind. Both scenarios lead to a visibly better situation afterwards.

THE SIXES: THE SINGER

The Singer communicates with others and creates experiences. They have a message and need it to be understood by an audience. The two parts of this process are both very important. It is not enough to speak your message out loud and not care if it was received by the listener; real communication doesn't finish until the other person knows what you were trying to say.

The Singer is a very public figure who creates joy and spectacle all projected outward. Actors and musicians fall into this Role, as does anyone who needs to make a speech to a crowd. The Singer is very much about seeking personal fame but also about feeling good while doing it. Music can be beautiful and sharing it with others is a happy experience.

Where the Warrior acts in opposition to something in society, the Singer projects energy into a grateful crowd and joins their celebration.

The Magician's Journey sees this step as the first time we discover the joy that having an adoring crowd can bring. This forces us to think about our self-image but also the image we want to project to the public. The Singer's valuable lessons are of finding authenticity in what you want to share, not just giving an audience whatever will bring you fame. The best communication requires thought, but adding true passion to your message will elevate it (and you) above the crowd.

SIX OF CLUBS: SINGER'S PROMISE
"CLAIRE READS A SECRET"

Communication, Written Messages, Being Understood

"My dearest sister—"

(What? That wasn't like Patrick at all. He hardly even called her Claire, it was usually "pan-face" or "porridge-head." Something was going on.)

"I am writing to you from the wonderful Haversham Correctional Home for Boys."

(Oh, so that was it.)

"I have behaved quite badly, and so am determined to redeem myself with good behavior according to the rules of this fine establishment. They are always fair here, and I am put in mind of the justice and education provided to us by our beloved schoolteacher, Mr. Thomas."

(Mr Thomas used to shout and hit his desk with a long ruler while going rather red in the face. Of course, no one else reading the letter would know that. Patrick was speaking directly to her.)

"While it's true that I haven't made the best start, I find myself remembering the lessons we learnt in Sunday school, and know that I will be much improved in the near future."

(Pat had lasted two hours at Sunday School before climbing out of the window and spending the day at the beach, picking up seashells. He was obviously going to break out of this place too. She checked the address: it was next to a pebble beach. That's where he would be.)

"The staff have suggested that my stay here be at least a year, and I replied that it is certainly what I deserve."

(Which is not the same as agreeing to stay.)

"For now I shall make a go of things, and wait out my time as patiently as old farmer O'Connor."

(Farmer O'Connor once kicked in his own barn door because he wouldn't wait thirty seconds for his son to bring the key. The escape would be as soon as possible, so she'd have to be ready tonight.)

"I hope you are well and still living with your friend and her sister."

(Bring two people.)

"See you when I see you,

Patrick."

("See you when I see you" was what their father used to say, every morning when he went to work. Since he returned at precisely six o'clock every evening, it meant … see you at precisely six o'clock.)

Claire put the letter down and began making the arrangements.

The Singer's Promise is Communication. Promise cards are about intention and plans, and the Singer wants to be heard. As the introduction to this Role states, there are two parts to successful communication: you must say what you mean *and* your audience must also understand it. A singer might want to make their audience feel sad with a melancholy song, but that will only work if the people think that the music and words are sad instead of happy. Communication is therefore about connecting properly with someone else so that you both view things the same way.

The Singer places a lot of importance on appearances. They stand up in public and are seen. They project energy and sound outward to influence people. However, for the first time in the Roles, there is also something more. Music, and all the other sounds that vibrate in air such as speech, can lift us out of normal life. A singer needs to sound genuinely caught up in the emotion of their song and finds a state of joy and serenity when doing so. No one becomes a singer just to convey words—a good one creates and also lives joyously in the song they make.

This card can signify that the reader will soon receive a message. In traditional playing card divination, this would be a written letter on paper, although these days it is just as likely to be an email. It is also a reminder that any important communication you make needs to be received correctly by its audience and that the words should not be misunderstood or ignored. To any "How do I achieve this?" questions, "communication" is an easily understood answer and always a good idea.

The other main meaning of the card is to tell the reader to use more communication. Again, it's difficult to think of any situation where this would be a bad move. Relationships can always use more of it; other problems can become easier if you bring someone else in on them. What's called for here is more than just dry speech, however. Look for ways to feel the Singer's performance and self-belief. Make the communications not just clear but meaningful.

The Promise Roles imagine the best version of their theme, and in communication that goes beyond logical words on a page: the Singer should aim to have the listener feel the emotions in their heart that prompted them to craft a message in the first place.

SIX OF DIAMONDS:
SINGER'S GAMBIT
"THE LADY OF THE FOREST"

Performance, Outward Appearances, Being Seen

When the world was younger than it is now, the Lady of the Forest strode through the woodland singing her song. As the breezes carried her sweet melody, the flowers around her opened and trees unfurled their leaves. Sunlight sent gentle slanting rays through the ranks of oak, elm and ash. The Lady placed her feet carefully along the sides of sparkling streams and ponds, tending to weeping willow and fiery alder.

She raised the note of her song to cause delight, and bright daffodils heard the call. From the busy undergrowth golden buttercups rose up in her steps and a carpet of bluebells covered a clearing when she passed.

Turning her voice to darkness, the Lady sang nightshade and holly and monkshood. She created shadowed groves of long-lived yew and quiet mounds where mushrooms slept.

All along her path the creatures of the forest gathered to listen and to peek out in wonder. Deer and wild horses, badgers and owls, beetle and squirrel and bat. They heard the music in their blood and were lifted by it, enchanted as the pure voice rang out to the stars and down to the mosses.

The Lady walked alongside a waterfall, and for the first time a tiny shiver entered her voice. It sang of caves which had collapsed, swamps fallen to rot. Those listening were confused, wondering how the Lady could fear that her work would not be perfect. Surely one so divine would have the power to guarantee her notes remained clear and life-giving? That changed when they saw her pass by, for her glamour was such that it was impossible to imagine this being as anything but perfect. And yet the tone of sadness and caution in her voice remained.

When she finally went on her way, leaving all observers behind, the sun seemed to dim and the streams quieten their splashing. But the forest itself and all life within it could still hear the piercing notes of her song, and it remembered them.

The Gambit cards are always the actions a Role takes. For the Singer, it is (unsurprisingly) to put on a performance but what this means in the modern day is quite complicated! We live in a time where the picture we would like to show of ourselves to the outside world is often different to our real life, especially on social media. This is also true of singers who find it useful to craft a persona for the stage and transport us to a world where glamor is possible (compared to earlier the same morning when they were half asleep with bed-hair and couldn't find their keys). A performance is an artificial time created to have maximum effect, but its artificiality doesn't make it bad. All the deliberate effort does succeed in making a performance more effective.

Another aspect of performing is being seen and judged. It can be a scary experience, whether you are speaking in public or using your charisma to convince just one person of something important. If you are performing, you will not be able to escape the spotlight.

There are three main things to consider when this card appears. In addition to "you will need to perform to make this happen" and "you will be seen; there's nowhere to hide," the Singer is also the first Role that steps into new territory: this card has a strong theme of losing yourself in the song. At the same time as wanting to sing for an audience, part of the Singer's journey is that they can close their eyes and lose themselves in a timeless moment.

Singers put part of their real selves into their music. After the earlier Roles of finding a goal, relating to people, creating and gaining security, and opposing those we disagree with, the Singer is the first to look inside and find a purer way to be. Though they seek the audience's approval, they also have an inner connection essential to moving forward in life.

The performance aspect of this card frequently refers to using skill in communication (the Singer's type of performance) and can mean impressing people at a meeting, performing in an exam, or anything where you must rise to the occasion of being tested and seen by others.

SIX OF SPADES:
SINGER'S FOLLY
"JENNY BUYS ANOTHER ROUND"

Celebration, Holiday, Carefree Enjoyment

"Jenny, are you in here?" The tavern room was crowded and noisy, but it was easy enough to find the young woman sat at a table—she was shouting while thrusting a tankard of ale into the air.

"Marcus, darling! Meet my very good friends Tom, Bob, and … sorry, what was his name again?" She gestured to the others around the table, but the third "friend" was loudly snoring and couldn't be woken to ask.

"Jenny, where have you been?" Marcus asked. "They said you rented a room here, but when I went there it was locked and there was a loud screaming noise inside."

"Oh yes, that's the peacock. Don't tell the landlord."

"The … Jenny, you were supposed to be home after your performance to meet the new priest when he came to the house."

"Stop being so serious and have a drink. That's not for ages yet!"

"It was last Wednesday."

The woman shrugged and emptied her tankard. "Listen, you won't believe it. I sang for the Earl's son and he paid me … oh, it was so much money! All the people said how good I was, and then he instructed his man to give me a huge sum in pounds!"

Marcus was clearly taken aback by this news. "Goodness Jen, that's wonderful! But you decided to celebrate in a tavern?"

"No, first I bought a puppy."

"A ... listen, Jen, you need to come home. I'm happy for you, but you have duties."

"Yes, yes. I will. I'm just going to order another roast dinner and ... some more ale, isn't that right my friends?" At this, a ragged cheer went up from the slumped figures around the large wooden table, and Marcus pinched the bridge of his nose in annoyance.

This stage of the Magician's Journey brings a frivolous, easy celebration, and is one of the nicest cards to receive in the deck. It's unusual for a Folly, which (while they're not automatically negative) are certainly full of problems in most of the Roles. The Folly of the Singer is that after a successful performance they can believe the outward appearances of their own glory, and ride on the wave of appreciation from the crowd. Celebrating then becomes easy.

This situation is actually fine and brings real relaxation, a very valuable thing in today's society. There is a cheery and optimistic holiday attitude to this card, one of sunny beaches and free time. You will be able to drop any stress you're feeling and really appreciate the break—the only drawback is that you won't get any work done. If you have pressing deadlines this means that it may be difficult to keep them when faced with other temptations.

This card is usually a bright ray of sunshine, unless it's in the middle of a lot of "you must do the hard work now!" messages. Then you might want to look at taking steps to ensure you can keep disciplined for the important task. At any other time, sit back and enjoy the relaxed happiness that the celebration brings.

If your question was regarding the best way to achieve something, the answer is that you should be as relaxed and happy as possible. Events will either take care of themselves or be so undemanding that you can easily guide them without any stress.

SIX OF HEARTS:
SINGER'S TRIUMPH
"LISSA SINGS OF LOVE AND SORROW"

Persuasion, Fame, Glamor

Lissa stood in the centre of the stage, waiting for the audience to fall silent. She started her performance singing the story of Nalia the orphan girl, growing up with her best friend Henki, supporting each other during the tense times of the previous years. It was a popular tale and the musical notes were plain and reassuring, letting the crowd feel the loyalty between the friends and their determination to survive hardships.

Then she sang of the sudden appearance of Dina and the fierce love that Nalia felt for them, and how she felt that Dina enriched her heart and brought colour to the world. At this the people in the room sighed, and as the notes soared pure and lightly, they remembered their own loves or held hands with the partner next to them.

Next Lissa moved on to the war, which swept Nalia out into the countryside. This song was a sad one indeed. The lovers were separated, and even her friendship with Henki was tested as so many changes came upon them both so quickly. Lissa sang of how in the countryside Nalia met Kon the Riddle-Master ... unknow-

able, unpredictable Kon, who taught her many mysteries. But this new knowledge was not enough to stop the pain of separation, and the singer's voice which rang out into the hall brought tears to the eyes of everyone there as it lamented the darkness that comes from being apart from a heart which belongs to you.

That's when she knew she had them. It was one thing to tell a tale for others to hear but another for them to truly know the emotions and to feel them within their own bodies. "If you can reach out and change people in that way," she thought to herself, "they are yours—and if you cannot then you are simply a bird singing outside the window, ignored and temporary."

For the finale, Lissa brought the unexpected but happy conclusion: Nalia and Dina reunited, their love strong. Henki who survived the early years with her friend's help, grown to be powerful and brilliant in the new age. And a voice which rose and rose to bring hope, first to the few characters, then their village, then their lands, and finally the real world that the audience occupied with all their own hopes and fears. The people would go home emboldened, uplifted, and she smiled as she felt the same during their ecstatic applause.

As the Singer deals in communication, their Triumph is to change the emotions and decisions of others. This is the Singer's masterwork: to use their voice to show others how the world can be, and to change listeners with their message. Successful persuasion is different from communication, the meaning of Singer's Promise. Simple communication is like receiving a letter from someone else, although it's better if you can share your real motivations as part of it. Persuasion is a much deeper and more rewarding connection, usually achieved by opening your heart a little and asking them to do the same.

A Singer who can convince their audience to do this will receive fame and adoration in return. This attention is not the same as the solemn gratitude the Healer earns, based on recognition of the person's real character. The Singer's fame is instead the glamor and illusion of a celebrity on a stage, a song of deeds and loves more intense than normal life. We saw in the Singer's Gambit that a singer (or famous actor or other artist) is not perceived as their real selves by the audience. Their outward appearance is accepted instead of the truth. The reward of such a performance is fame, but not a very deep or personal one. It isn't related directly to the work done so much as it is the people's excitement for anybody in the spotlight.

When this Triumph appears in a reading, it first of all is about persuasion. It also implies that the situation will gain you wider popularity. Despite the maybe shallow nature of fame, it's often difficult to see how this would ever be a bad thing. The one obvious answer is if you were trying to keep a secret or hide from someone; in that case, it may be far too much attention at a time when you don't want it.

Fame isn't the only reason that a Singer sings. In the journey of the Roles, they have moved on from being alone, finding a partner, choosing how to face society, earning a trade, deciding what they stand for and what they oppose, and now the Singer sings because … they want to. Even the most attention-seeking celebrity needs to have at least a little bit of this desire. They perform for the joy and for what art brings to other people. Whether a serious calling or just a leisure activity, singing needs to feel good and be about connecting to something larger than oneself. This connection to a brighter inner world is something that we will see again later with the Dancer, but the Singer is the first to try it and to perform it for others.

This Triumph is the conclusion of a very extroverted set of cards: talking to others, performing under pressure, loud enjoyment, and deliberate persuasion while in the spotlight. This collection of extrovert actions ends with one that signifies noise and attention but also guarantees a typical Triumph's good outcome.

THE SEVENS: THE NOBLE

The Singer's fame leads to money and influence, and naturally to the Role of the Noble. This Noble is not a king, queen, or princess—all the gendered names have too many associations of more power or less. Instead, this title applies instead to everyone who has any power over others. As with all the Roles, it applies to any gender.

You might not think that "money and influence" sounds like you. Most of us don't feel as though we're rich or powerful compared to those around us, and indeed we might be struggling to gain money, respect, or basic security. However, most of us will be involved with making some decisions for another person, even if on a very small level. This could take the form of you asking someone to trust your leadership, or to accept your version of events. It might be others asking you to take the lead in even a small matter. Whatever it is, most of us will experience responsibility for others at some point.

There's nothing wrong with being in a position of power over someone else, provided it is completely consensual. Having a decision-maker for a group can be useful and efficient … but it comes with challenges, and the Role of the Noble explores these. After previously tasting fame on the Magician's Journey as the Singer, the lessons now turn to the responsibility that comes with that power. Obligations at home, questions on how you will use the control you have over others, and wrestling with your ego are all part of discovering worldly power.

SEVEN OF CLUBS:
NOBLE'S PROMISE
"LADY MAPENZI FACES THE STORM"

Home, Fair Dealing, Contentment

"Get inside the house, go!"

The storm continued to roar around them, and the children ran for the cover of the main building.

"Lady Mapenzi, please, we must save the stables! Lightning has started a fire. We'll lose everything on that side."

"Are the horses free?"

"Yes, they've run to the far fields, but the building—"

"There are still people who need help on the road, come with me now."

The tall woman swept forward into the rain, the night sky thrashing above and winds sending bushes tumbling along the ground. Her house was stronger than any around it and should survive the storm easily enough, but many others had lost their shelter already. The girl who ran alongside her was talking of the stables again, but Mapenzi cut her off with a loud shout to new figures whom they met in the darkness.

"Biran! Get to the house!"

"Bless you, Lady." The man and his family hurried up the road past them as more lightning struck nearby. The girl tried again.

"But the stables! And the kitchens! These people can find their own—"

Mapenzi turned on her, much taller and with a voice full of command.

"You seem to think that these are my buildings. They are not. They belong to the people. I serve the villagers. I might spend my time meeting diplomats instead of bringing in the crops, but that doesn't mean I deserve riches and they don't. People are more important than houses, Sibo, and that building is theirs to use."

The small girl stood gaping up at her leader as howling winds tore at their clothing.

"Now, back to the main room. It is strong with good foundations. There are two families I haven't seen yet, so I must go and search."

Mapenzi pulled up the hood of her cloak and strode into the night.

The promise that the Noble makes to those who serve them is to use the power and money they gain from the position to provide everyone with a stable home. Others consenting to give you power over them is an exchange— they need to get something back. In most societies around the world, this exchange is broken. The rich have far, far more than the poor agreed for them to have and do not provide the safety from poverty or fair reward for work that should be given in such situations. If a Noble has people working on their land and giving power to them, but those workers do not have a reliable home, then the contract is not being honored. The Role usually works on a smaller scale because most of us won't actually be a member of a noble house (nor do we live in a feudal society), but it also applies to any time we make decisions on behalf of other people.

That decision making for others is something that can happen quite often to any of us. It might be in tiny ways, but we will all eventually have to take responsibility for someone else. It is part of growing up, and a crucial step in working out who we are in the world.

The first meaning when the Noble's Folly is revealed is usually related to domestic matters, as this card in particular deals with the one place where some have power over others—the home. Home is a huge and important part of everyone's lives no matter how they live. Security and shelter, somewhere to belong, privacy, and a place to rest are essentials for everyone's wellbeing.

This is a brilliant card for all dealings with authority, as it predicts benevolent and fair behavior according to agreed-upon rules. A Noble's Promise is the ideal everyone wishes would be delivered, the well-intentioned words before any compromises must be made. It is full of positivity and sincerity from those who have power over us, whether that's parents, teachers, bosses, or politicians.

This particular Role is also the first on the Magician's Journey that implies a duty paired with every part of the Role's experience. There is one right way to be a Noble: to be responsible to those from whom you benefit.

If this card is addressing something that will happen in the future, it's already a success and the person has got that balance right. If it's drawn as an instruction on how to act, the message is to be immediately humble and make sure you are treating those around you fairly. Are others doing emotional or physical work you're taking for granted? Is there someone who can't make the changes they want because you're in control of that part of the picture and ignoring them?

The Promise's idealist nature will win in most scenarios, making this a statement that the Noble acted properly and the result is a calm and content home, appreciation and respect from others, and harmony with those closest to you.

SEVEN OF DIAMONDS: NOBLE'S GAMBIT
"OMOREDE IS NOT ALONE"

Friendship, Loyalty, Recognising Debts

Omorede sat at the desk in the nearly empty room and looked at the dust all around. This place had been his home for many years, but now there was no one left to help, and no way he would be able to keep it. He didn't know where he would go next.

Ewansiha entered and leant against the doorframe. He crossed his arms, smiling down at his old friend. "I see you're taking this well."

The older man was startled, and the surprised expression stayed on his face when he recognised who had spoken. "Ewansiha? What are you doing here?"

"I decided to stay."

There was a pause as Omorede checked that he'd heard the words correctly.

"But it's so much money! You can't turn that down."

"Of course I can. You didn't think...?" He walked in and sat on the edge of the wooden desk. "Do you remember when my niece was sick, and you sat by her bed so that I could work?"

"We didn't know if she'd live, but now she's moved to the islands with a family of her own."

"Yes. And when the flood came, you remember how you helped us clear the street?"

"Of course."

"And when I thought that it would be a really good idea to trust a business partner in the city, and they nearly took everything? You gave me the money."

Omorede was silent now. His friend continued: "I would have lost my own home at least once if not for you. Asking around, I'm not the only one. So, I'm not going to leave you behind for something like money. I'd have none at all if you hadn't helped, again and again."

Looking into the distance, Ewansiha became thoughtful. "I could be swimming in profit next month but surrounded by people I don't respect ... I'd rather have enough to get by, but keep supporting the people here. And you."

Silently, Omorede reached out and grasped his friend's hand tightly. Ewansiha grinned. "So, don't bother packing, we're all going to help you keep this place."

There are many cards symbolizing luck in this deck; sometimes it's bad luck, and there is even an entire Role for the Trickster. On the other side from this unpredictable chaos is the loyalty of friends, holding the situation together and working to stabilize anything that causes us fear.

Loyalty and true friendship are the answers to many of the typical questions asked in divination. "Can I trust this person?" "Is this person lying to me?" "If I take this action, will I lose my friends?" To these questions and more, this card is a reassuring and firm message of strong friendship.

It can also go beyond friendship. Loyalty can mean loyalty to a superior in a situation where you are under pressure to betray them. It can mean choosing sides, or working hard when you would rather take the easy route. This card can show a debt owed, one that requires careful thought.

In the Magician's Journey, it is here the Noble draws on the loyalty of their people and risks abandonment. Loyalty is the currency Nobles use to get things done, but that loyalty needs to be earned and they need to be trusted. The card is usually reassuring when it says that friendship will hold true. After all, this isn't casual friendship or the wider society the Healer deals with—it is the work of the Noble and the question of whether they have power to make things happen or not. Nobles rely on other people for that power, so what's being are tested the links to those people. It could be personal friendship but it's much more often people over whom you have some kind of power.

Not many of us are a queen, an office manager, or a captain in an army. We don't have people reporting directly to us; we just have friends, family, and colleagues we can ask for help or who have some sort of small obligation to us. They could simply be people whose help we need for a personal project or even a hobby, as long as they are following our directions. This is the kind of link many of us have to the Noble, but just because it's not an official title doesn't mean it is of smaller importance. The Noble is a vital Role for everyone, because it covers what we do when we have power.

Being in the position of power and then trying to use it is always a risk. The people you thought were reliable might not be. You could fail in holding up your end of the deal, in treating people properly, or doing enough planning. Power is difficult; being honest about what we owe to others is something that will always reward us.

This card puts the net of power that the Noble commands into action. It tells us to call on others for help, to explore how well we handle being given power over other people and to make big decisions based on being in a position of responsibility.

SEVEN OF SPADES:
NOBLE'S FOLLY
"TATIANA, QUEEN OF THE WORLD"

Ego, Prejudice, Injustice

"Mighty one, I am Tatiana, Queen of all from East to West, the supreme leader of the Empire, owner of palaces, cities, and the largest army the world has ever seen. My glory is known across every land and my enemies fear my very name. Each morning trained servants wash my hair with purest water and perfumes, and my clothes are adorned with famous jewels. Truly, I am the only one worthy to meet your challenge."

Far above Tatiana stood the goddess of her people, whose hair was made of night mists and mountain streams, whose eyes were burning stars, whose arms were rolling green hills and lush meadows. When she leant forward to regard the mortal, deserts shivered and bright sunshine burst from clear crystals. Her voice was rain upon lily ponds and hot thunder over ancient trees.

"Mortal. Tell me the extent of your rights over others."

The Queen raised her head proudly and smiled. "My command of the people is absolute. When a province defied my rule, I sent my army to burn their towns and enslave their leaders. All beneath me must pay gold to my collectors, and my word is law."

The goddess shifted, birds flying from treetops and winds howling through ravines.

"No. You have no rights over others. Be silent and listen."

Tatiana had been about to object but closed her mouth with a scowl. The voice before her dropped in volume to the flutter of bats escaping a cave, of soft sunlit waves over sand.

"Mortal, my champion must know the true cost of their actions and feel the changes that they make in the world. When they step, all the rock beneath them is aware of it. When they move a hand, they push aside the air. Their actions are felt by everything that is. The taking of a whole life should be enough to devastate the champion's mind and senses forever. But you do not know this. You do not see those who are in your power as people. In your reasoning they are not equal to you. They have become resources to be used. You do not feel their pain as your own."

The eyes of the goddess, hanging in the air before the tiny woman, were so vast and full of love and wisdom—but now they narrowed as quickly as shadows filling a forest.

"I have no use for a champion who cannot feel."

And then the ground was falling away, and the shining gold and gems hung upon Tatiana's silks, the heavy crown and all her armies were not enough to save her.

The Noble cards so far have shown how Nobles should act, and what they hope for in return. The Folly is the opposite of all the ways that they "should" act. It is instead a list of the dangers that power brings.

The biggest danger is ego. Society tells us that the person with the most money, property, or power over others is one who is better than any who are poorer. When we have those things, we believe that we rise in status and have succeeded in life. This is a natural place for the Noble, who by definition is above other people in some way. When our self-importance rises, so does our sense of personal identity or the idea that we are separate to everyone else. It is easy to go from there to the belief that "*my* needs are more important."

You are not superior to any other human. Your wants and needs don't override theirs, and your identity doesn't give you more rights than them … except in many cultures it often does, and the messages we receive (both loudly and quietly) are that some people deserve to have power over others.

Nobles quickly move from valuing all people less to being more specific in who to see as expendable. Racism and sexism come from choosing one group to be more and one to be less. No child is born racist or sexist; it is taught to them by adults and societies that show that anyone who is different from you can be excluded. The Role of the Noble (which includes all of us in some aspect of our lives, even if it's just when we communicate with children) has the power to do the most damage with this, and so people in that Role should never act on prejudice.

Ego leads to "us and them," which leads to exclusion and injustice. However, a sense of your own identity can also be useful. It is linked to self-respect, and feelings of our own worth. You are not more important than other people—but neither are you less important. Many of us tolerate behavior toward ourselves that we wouldn't if we saw it elsewhere. If that harmful behavior was happening to a friend, we would tell that friend it was unfair and that they should not accept it … but when it happens to us, we allow it.

If this card appears, your first reaction should be to check that your own ego has not been making you behave badly. The second reaction should be the opposite, to check that you have been using your ego as much as you deserve to.

Humility is something all Nobles could use more of. The Healer showed that compassion for others goes a long way, but an essential further step is the manner in which we think about ourselves. No matter the temptations of the Noble—money, fame, status—we all need to remember that everyone is important.

SEVEN OF HEARTS:
NOBLE'S TRIUMPH
"DALTON'S EMPTY ADVICE"

Searching for Answers, Continuing
Responsibility, Restlessness

"How many people want to see me, Dalton?"

"A crowd of around forty, sir. More than yesterday."

"I see. What do you think is the purpose of life, Dalton? I've been wondering."

"I'm sure I have no idea, sir. Here is the list of petitions for this morning, and this stack of papers over here as well."

"It's just that having the extra money doesn't seem to help. It used to feel good to solve people's problems, but now…there are always more problems. I thought being rich would make it more tolerable, but it hasn't."

"I'm sorry to hear that, sir. The ambassador is waiting in the main hall, she has rejected your latest trade offer."

"What kind of music would I make, do you think, if I learned the lute?"

"I'm sure I don't know, sir. You told me to remind you of the issue in the village—the Carter family is demanding the return of their land from the Mayners, and the head of the Mayner house

says they will kill every living Carter before that happens. The Bishop wrote to say that if you don't resolve the dispute by tomorrow, the Church will confiscate the entire area and the plot next to it as well."

"I've never been to the big lake on the other side of the mountains, Dalton. I want to see what the water looks like on a winter morning. I always meant to experience more of nature at sunrise."

"That's very nice, sir. The treasury is doing well after your quick action last month but has reported that it will need assistance this month as well or we won't be able to buy enough food when the harvest comes in."

The richly dressed man sat in his elegant chair and wished with all his heart that he could be somewhere else. Anywhere else, really.

The problem with being a Noble (and therefore being responsible for others) is that the challenges never end. You do not reach a place where you stop being afraid of the dangers that could disrupt home, family, or those who look to you for leadership.

The other issue the Noble faces is encountered only by those who think that seeking power, wealth, and control are all you need to do in life. As soon as they have those things, they realize that they do not give real security or fulfil our hopes in the way that society promises. You can chase money, items, fame or sensations, but soon they will not be enough. Even people who are extremely rich never think that they have enough—they look at the few still above them and feel they need to compete further. The struggle never stops.

Many of us are Nobles in small ways when we take on responsibility for other people at work or in the home. We too can find the job of keeping those people safe and prosperous doesn't end. Even if we enjoy the challenge or welcome the responsibility, the work only covers some aspects of life. Focusing excessively on just the Noble Role leaves us with questions: what about our inner life? Who would we be without these obligations, if we had more time? Is there more to experience in life than chasing money or power? Even at its ultimate point, the Role of the Noble can leave us dissatisfied.

This is one of the rare Triumph cards which is not totally positive. In a reading, it shows restless frustration and ongoing duties. It can also mean shortsightedness in terms of the big things: believing that money and possessions are all that matter instead of searching properly within for what might fulfil you.

On the other hand, it is a Triumph, which means that tasks associated with the Noble Role will continue to go very well. If the reader is concerned with control of decisions, respect from others or a well-run household, this card certainly provides those. There is a lot of comfort and even luxury. It *is* easy to simply keep going when things are fine. But if we stay in that comfortable space, they may never be better than fine.

The Noble shows a lot of what society tells us is important in life. If you have succeeded at the Noble Role, you might think that there's nowhere else to go from there. But this essential restlessness is what pushes us on to look further, deeper, and in different places than the demands of power would steer us toward.

In the Magician's Journey, it is at this point the Noble rejects what they have built. They reached out to society as the Healer, learned a skill and decided what they would fight for, gained fame as the Singer, and used that fame to build power as the Noble. It all led to one point, so why stop? The answer is that the Noble gives you power, but also responsibility you may not want, as well as respectability you must live up to. It takes up all your time and doesn't satisfy your mind or heart. It leads the Noble to think, "is this all there is?"

When they reach a crisis point, the Noble will reject their wealth, possessions, and status and take a new road in a search for answers. That is what the card indicates: domestic and public success but the need to look to your more spiritual needs as well.

THE EIGHTS: THE HERMIT

After the fame of the Singer and political power of the Noble, most people expect to be happy, but that is often not how things turn out! We are taught to seek money and influence, but if we get them, they can surprise us by being very unsatisfying.

The Singer's Fame is based on external glamour, the Noble's power is over physical resources or people. There is another part of life we must explore if we are to reach the wisdom necessary to become the Magician, and it is entirely internal.

The Hermit gives us the route to reach this new knowledge through travel, peace, and silence. They realize that everything they have gained up to now in life isn't enough, so they take time away from daily pressures to look inside and find a better way to be.

As part of the whole journey, this retreat stage is a famous one. Everyone needs to do it at some point. Either you will be dissatisfied with life and want to make changes, or you might find a spiritual or mental challenge that requires silence and solitude to think and reflect upon so that you can move to better things.

Silence can be a powerful tool for self-improvement, but the overall message of the Hermit is that you are not your job or your fame; achieving status in society is not enough. Humans need more than that in order to have inner peace and inner strength. To reach the heights of the later Roles, concentrating on your inner needs is absolutely necessary.

EIGHT OF CLUBS:
HERMIT'S PROMISE
"SARA REACHES THE EMPTY SKY"

Travel, Peace, Escape

Sara put both hands on the rock and pulled herself up the last part of the steep slope. Behind her lay the winding path from the base of the mountain. The journey had not been tiring, and her spirit was light and happy. Now she had come to the narrow passageway that divided these lands from the next.

A few moments of pushing through the gap between the crevice walls, turned sideways to slip as carefully as she could between the high stone barrier on either side, only a few moments of darkness and held breath, and then she was through.

Sara gasped at the change. Strong sunlight warmed a vast open space. A wide valley, full of fields and streams, stretched out below her in a bowl that extended to the horizon. The empty sky above was a pale blue with drifts of white cloud. She could feel the winds moving freely around the mountain peak, the fresh breeze bringing new scents. A falcon soared above, crying suddenly into the soft quiet.

Smiling in achievement, Sara sat with her back to the sheer rock wall and felt something in her unclench for the first time in a long while. There were no people here, no noisy demands. She closed her eyes and listened to the slow winds and the lone bird, her smile only growing.

The idea of escaping from it all to spend time alone is a seductive one. The Hermit's Promise is of quiet restfulness, fresh air, and a place to relax. When we leave all the pressures of the day behind, we can think clearly and without distraction.

This card strongly suggests travel, but it doesn't have to be physical travel to another location. The theme is more along the lines of "getting away from the noise" to find a place where you can think in peaceful quiet. Travel itself is often described as a way to escape our worries, but it rarely works (we do, after all, bring our head with us to the new place). That said, everyone needs the potential benefit of escaping from stress and leaving everyday life behind so that we can relax and remember who we are.

Escape is essential now and then. You are not your job, your grades, or your reputation with friends. The demands of normal life are difficult, and occasional escape from them is healthy and fun.

The Hermit doesn't have to be entirely alone during this time but they do need to be able to operate without any intense connections clouding their mind. The goal of travelling is to be able to think deeply and seriously at the other end, and distance can help with that.

If this card appears in a reading that is otherwise filled with stress or danger, it doesn't mean frantically running away—this travel is always deliberate. It is something you control and leads to a slow, peaceful relaxation. Most often the message will be to make your mind entirely calm and work out the answer without fear, or it will refer to a need to put distance between yourself and the sources of stress. This distance can be mental, as simple as time spent alone in a quiet room; it doesn't mean you need to leave the country! In fact, escape from mental turmoil is one of the most common meanings.

Promise cards are often perfect imaginings of the best a Role can offer, and here the Hermit delivers contentment, peace, and rest.

EIGHT OF DIAMONDS:
HERMIT'S GAMBIT
"HEDDA SPEAKS TO THE ANCESTORS"

Mental Effort, Clarity, Ignoring Interruptions

Hedda sat in the cave, looking out at the bright morning. A wooden staff lay on the stone floor in front of her, but she didn't reach for it yet.

The staff was the property of the Speaker, the one who communed with the ancestors. It was her duty to take it up, but every time she lifted it and listened for their voices she was overcome by emotion—grief for those who had gone before, shame from being unable to help her people in the way she should.

Hedda listened to the silence in the cave, which was broken only by far-off animals and the quiet sounds of nature. Her fingers touched the staff. Immediately, the storm of emotion returned: low and high voices disrupting her concentration. She imagined her family accusing her of failing and added that to the wave of guilt. Once more, she pushed it all away and dropped the relic, cursing.

When her heartbeat had slowed again, the young woman thought deeply. Nature continued its murmurings outside but all else was still. She had come here to escape the gaze and judgement of her people, and she was indeed alone now, but it was not enough. Running from her grief did not work and numbing herself to it simply removed any other connection she could make. It wasn't possible to only numb one part, it deadened everything— including the senses she needed to call on now.

Hedda was carrying the sadness in her body like a physical token, but the mind is not the body. The mind could instead create a place where only the actions required by her duty existed. An empty space in which she was powerful enough, resolute enough to find a way forward.

Finally, she lifted the wooden staff once more and let the voices come. They surrounded her like an angry wind, shouting and demanding. She kept entirely still, searching with a mind that was shaped like a needle. Through the voices and the pain. Through the uncertainty and self-doubt. She had a right to be here and a duty to fulfil. It seemed as though she flew among clouds, but this time they did not distract her from the straight journey she insisted on. Her eyes were closed, face blank, and her breathing did not quicken.

With her mind strong, calm and her own, she reached out for her ancestors and immediately heard a warm and loving voice in return.

"Hello, Daughter."

The Hermit takes a break from the expansion of many of the previous Roles. Escaping society, they remove all distractions of the heart and body to focus entirely on the mind. When a problem requires solving, they are able to use their mind to its fullest extent.

This gives the Hermit amazing clarity. They can see the situation as it really is and make decisions without emotion. The wisdom that comes from this can be profound. If this card is drawn, it advises the reader to concentrate and solve the problem using thought rather than action or strong emotions. It is often the card of academic work.

Depending on the other cards that appear with it, Hermit's Gambit can give advice (e.g., that you should be logical instead of emotional) or a warning (e.g., that you are being too remote and not emotional enough!). The Hermit's way involves isolating yourself from life's noise and false pressures … but this can go too far. In particular, running away from fear instead of facing it isn't healthy, and making decisions very coldly can lead to trouble. As much as the Hermit wants to control them, emotions are valuable guides that tell us why we act the way we do. Emotions have the potential to connect us to others and help us remember those who will be affected by our actions.

Every Gambit is a risk; the tightrope the Hermit walks is to find just the right amount of distance and peace. Negative emotions such as anger and hate can lead us to make terrible decisions, where seeing the situation more clearly could reveal that a problem never came from the source at which the anger is aimed. If we overly rely on logic, it can reduce everything to a calculated trade. People become numbers we can justify harming, or we numb ourselves to emotion so much that we don't feel beneficial emotions we should be embracing.

In the modern world, many of us lead lives full of noise and worry. Clearing our head enough to solve a mental task is usually a very good thing. If we can't use our mental resources strongly, we may fail the Gambit—but if we go too far, we could end up entirely in our heads, assuming that cold logic has all the answers, disconnected from our bodies.

Use this card's opportunity to create a space where you can think without interruption, but when you have finished calculating, come back to your full self and check the results with an open heart.

EIGHT OF SPADES:
HERMIT'S FOLLY
"THE EMERALD MASK REPAID"

Isolation, Overthinking, Prioritising
Thoughts Over Deeds

The famed hero, "the Emerald Mask," was surrounded!

From all sides of the darkened warehouse, her enemy's allies closed in. There was no chance of fighting so many. She let her rapier fall to the ground. The sneering villain Lucia, "The Blade," took her time to savor the moment.

"So, Emerald Mask! You fall at last. I shall take your city, have your lover exiled to the mountains and finally see you defeated at my feet!"

The Mask made no reply. Around her, Lucia's crowd of brigands stood still, letting their leader set the pace of the encounter. Daggers and clubs waited in rough hands, handkerchiefs pulled up over each face.

The taunting continued: "Now you will be killed, alone and friendless. Your mighty skill with the sword will not save you this time. Have you any last words, before the end?"

In the silence that followed, in the final precious seconds, the beloved rogue known as The Emerald Mask looked straight into her enemy's eyes, and slowly asked the most important question of her life:

"Hey Lucia, where did you get your henchmen?"

This was not what The Blade had expected. Confused, she shrugged and answered: "The docks, mostly. Hired muscle, anyone who can hold a weapon and wanted to make some coin. Why?"

Under the shining green half-mask, our hero smirked and crossed her arms. "Because this is Venice. Here, spectacle creates legends. A name on the lips of the crowd becomes a hero known in every kitchen, on every street corner. And a villain who would attempt to kill The Emerald Mask will have to fight an entire city to do it."

The space around Lucia began to shrink as the dockhands and street brawlers silently turned around to face the villain and push her toward the doors.

"No! Stay away!" Lucia threatened first one, then another with the sharp tip of her sword, but she could not stop an entire room with no space to move. She was swept back by the crush of bodies, and out into the street.

The Mask recognised one of the men by her side. "Hello, Alfredo. How is your sister doing now that she has that medicine?"

"Much better, Emerald Mask. Thank you again."

One person wears the Mask, but they inspire a community. On some days, that unspoken contract between them is repaid.

The Hermit's Folly is Isolation. Humans are social animals, and while getting away from the noise to find solitude and peace often does us good in the modern world, it is difficult when it becomes your whole life. The Hermit can fall into the trap of believing that intellectual pursuits are all they need and that purely mental processes can provide all the answers—this isn't true!

We live in a very disconnected way from each other, even in cities. Despite hundreds of people in a small urban area (or maybe because of it) many people don't know their neighbors, and loneliness is very common. We need connection with others for all kinds of reasons, and taking the Role of the Hermit to an extreme level can be a block to achieving that.

When this card is encountered, it frequently means that you have tried to do something alone when you would be better off relying on friends. We often come to divination when we face challenges and a common reaction is to try to tackle them alone.

As usual, though, the situation you're reading this card within greatly affects the advice it gives. This card's meaning, "Isolation," and its being a Folly would usually suggest that you should beware of excess isolation and give thought to what you could achieve with friends. But if the problem is that too many people are already involved, the advice would be exactly the opposite, that your solution requires isolation. Others may be trying to influence your decision, or you may be unable to see it clearly with them so closely involved—in this case, the Hermit's ability to retreat and be alone is valuable. (Note that the Folly cards do not automatically mean that the idea they bring is a wrong one every time, only that it is a common flaw of the Role.)

Generally, there are more negative aspects to being isolated than positive ones. It's easy to overthink, to be too coldly unemotional, to feel rejected or unworthy when you are alone for long periods of time and do not have other people there to remind you of your connections. Sometimes it is useful to go somewhere quiet to think deeply, but frequently it is a mistake to cut ourselves off from others. Look carefully at whether there are individuals that you could stay away from, entire groups whose noise you need to leave behind for a short while, or whether you would benefit from bringing in more people instead. Look at whether you're overthinking things instead of seeking out a useful action to move them forward.

EIGHT OF HEARTS:
HERMIT'S TRIUMPH
"THE PHOENIX AND THE STARS"

Reconciliation, New Knowledge, Returning

The Phoenix of the southern sky meditated in silence. The stars of her wings and body shone their white light into the deep darkness, the wide spaces between each bringing quiet peace to her mind. Before her stood the door, the final portal to rejoin the world of people and animals, to regain her place in the heavens that could be seen by the mortals who looked up from their realm.

Crystalline light crossed the door in different colours, running in thin webs from one part of the frame to another. Occasionally, a new line would appear as the Phoenix made a connection in her thinking. Nothing moved for a time, until her Enemy appeared.

"You shall not gain the doorway."

Its voice was deep as a chasm into rock, its bulky form shimmered with fire and dark night. Pacing to the place where the Phoenix was sitting, it taunted her again.

"Stop. Your mind shall be clouded, your fears shall overcome thought. Anger and despair shall halt your progress."

The Phoenix gave no answer to this, but another connection on the doorway was linked by a precise line of colour.

"Stop. Your work cannot be perfected, for you are too weak. Life on the other side contains noise and obligation, expectations and confusion."

Still the Phoenix made no sound. Her mind was peaceful, and she had a task to complete.

"You were not ready before. You had fame and your place in the sky, and you have lost them. What can you be without others recognising your status?"

For the first time, the starbird replied.

"I do not require the praise of others. I have the strength of my mind."

The Enemy responded with fury. "You are alone! The heavens were too crowded for you, so you ran to hide in this place of secrets. Now you are friendless, and working to return? Foolishness!"

"What you say is true. I did retreat from my place, seeking silence. I had stared too long at the world of mortals, at its pressures and noise and evil deeds. I could not solve their problems or bring the quiet within myself. Soon, their struggle became mine. I am not a creature who can hold such things within."

With a shout of triumph, the Enemy advanced, only to stop at the next word.

"But then I rested here and spent time in thought. I was able to calm my mind and find a way to exist that does not fall to noise. When the woes of the mortals are hurled toward me, I can bend to avoid them. I can flow around them. I can see my own being distinct from them and maintain my silence."

"You should be afraid. By leaving, you have lost your family and locked yourself alone in this place forever."

"No. I am not alone."

And then that was true, because the door was complete. The last line of colour burned between the points, and suddenly around them her family appeared—the star bodies of the Crane and the Unicorn, the beautiful and immense Swan with eons between her white fires, and the Crow. The Enemy fled, and the wise bird retook her place in the skies holding new knowledge and peace within her being.

The Hermit achieves several things no other Role can. They draw on the experience of all the previous Roles to think deeply and carefully about matters. When this is successful in Hermit's Triumph, what they do with that knowledge changes them as a person in very good ways.

By moving away from the world and finding a private place, the Hermit is not distracted by other people's demands and can listen to their inner self. The applications of this knowledge are often also about the self. The biggest one is reconciliation, taking a problem and thinking it out logically until it can be dealt with and you are at peace with it. If there is hurt from a relationship, for example, this means looking realistically at what has actually been done and what is offered for the future—with your head, not your heart. The wisdom gained can be thought of as a key that unlocks a secret, or a light that dispels darkness. When this Triumph card appears, it means successfully finding an answer that previously eluded you.

After the Hermit's business is done, they will return to the real world and all of its demands—money, social interactions and relationships. These are things that the Hermit did not have to deal with during their retreat. However, they are not the same person they were previously: the new answers have changed them. They cannot go back to being the Singer or the Noble now. This means that even though the current surroundings look familiar, the person in them is different and this "return" is really a new beginning. Reconciliation is always a welcome result in a reading, and this is one of the most comforting Triumphs.

THE NINES: THE DANCER

The Dancer takes the wisdom they have learned in their time away as the Hermit and applies it to the physical life they have now returned to. Where before they struggled to achieve power or fame, as the Dancer they know what is truly important (and it is not either of those things). They don't fight the small details and so move through the world much less anxiously. They listen carefully to the cycles of nature and are carried along when those go in a useful direction.

The Dancer does not get into arm-wrestling matches with anyone. They move easily around obstacles and take whatever route will use less energy, avoiding instead of confronting unless the situation requires it. They wait for the right time to take advantage of the tide and prioritize their inner happiness above worldly demands. All of this comes naturally from their place in the Magician's Journey. They have been away as the Hermit and now refuse to live their life the way that they did before. Every moment becomes an opportunity to dance in a new way instead of just walk. Harmony becomes built into every minute.

There are still dangers, notably of losing oneself in the music instead of staying grounded, but this ninth Role is an exciting one. You have tried the different aspects of life and gained the wisdom you need. After this, only one final lesson needs to be learned.

NINE OF CLUBS:
DANCER'S PROMISE
"ADELISE LISTENS WITHIN"

Intuition, Connection, Avoiding Danger

"Oh yes, you are very powerful. I can sense that you know just the right one to pick! Which will it be?"

Adelise looked at the street stall in front of her with its three overturned cups and the man who sat behind it grinning. She reached out with her mind, trying to find which container called to her. She pointed to the one on the left and he leant forward to lift it. The ball was underneath!

A crowd who had gathered around the stall all clapped, and she felt a rush of excitement.

"Now, young lady, because you clearly have the gift, will you wager double the amount on one more try?"

There was a gasp and muttering from the people near her. That was suddenly a lot of money. She barely had that much, but if she won—oh, the things she could do if she won!

"What does your intuition tell you, which cup? Will you play?" He put the ball back under the one on the left and swapped them around too quickly for her to follow. She couldn't risk it. She

should only agree if she was sure she could feel which cup was the correct one.

Calming her mind and thinking hard again, Adelise examined how she felt about each of the choices. Not that one. No. Maybe that one?... Yes, surely it must be the middle cup! She should reach out and tell him she accepted the bet and—no. Something. Something's wrong.

Adelise knew it must be the one in the middle, but every time she decided to speak up a voice in her mind told her there was danger. She looked from the table to the faces of the stall owner and his assistant.

Why that cup? Why danger? She decided to pay heed to the warning and studied the people around her. The owner's eyes were too bright, he was too happy. He should be at least open to the possibility of losing, but look at him—totally confident. His breathing was too forceful, he wasn't sitting like he should be, everything was ... wrong in some way. She didn't like it.

Reaching out, she quickly overturned each of the three cups before he could move. They clattered to the street, all empty. The crowd were instantly furious, shouting at the stallholder—who grabbed up his wares and ran.

"Huh. I guess I do have a gift for this after all," thought Adelise.

The Hermit's purely mental approach works well if you have space and silence but can be difficult to maintain when surrounded by everyday noise. The Dancer takes a different route, feeling their way forward with emotion and intuition.

The point of learning the Dancer's wisdom is to make it easier to navigate through life. The Dancer knows that all the desires of the outside world are foolish: for power, or possessions, or recognition. You can spend all your time striving to gain those and be very unhappy doing it. Instead they create a calm mind and happy emotions and learn to avoid most of the unnecessary confrontation in the world. This is achieved through intuition and connection, which are related.

To explore our intuition we must first become more connected with the world. It is not solely an act of looking within, but of opening your perception to take in more details from outside. Intuition is not coldly logical—it's heavily emotional. A person walking down a street using their intuition to understand what can be seen is someone who has their senses fully open in order to gather information. This is not the same as the connection to a single other person the Lover discovers; it is between the self and the whole environment.

Our subconscious decisions keep us alive using instinct and collected knowledge. This card tells you to pay attention to intuition and look within for the answers. If something seems wrong to you about a situation or person, it probably is. Trust your instincts.

Equally, your own feelings about the outcome are more important than someone else's conclusions. If you ask a friend's opinion and they say no, but you think about it and decide yes, then you have been helped to see where your decision always was.

Living this way can bring depth and feeling while also helping us avoid the traps that many people fall into. Deliberately choosing to use intuition every day is a brave thing to do, and a rewarding one. It can protect against the shallow or false goals society tells us to desire and can reveal what actually matters to each of us. A Dancer who moves through life this way is very different from the earlier Roles who are more concerned with worldly power, such as the Singer and the Noble.

The Dancer's Promise is that your intuition will give the right answer for this question. Look inward and trust yourself.

NINE OF DIAMONDS:
DANCER'S GAMBIT
"ANJA ENTERS THE CAVE"

Cycles, Habits, Burdens

The Cave had always stood next to the village, its dark entrance issuing a silent challenge since before anyone's grandparents were born. Laws had been passed dictating that any person who would attempt to enter it must first give up their lands and power. This began as a test to prove that the candidate was not motivated by greed, but soon became useful to sort out matters of inheritance— those who went in rarely came out again.

Yesterday, Stefan had made the attempt. A huge man, he strode up to the darkened mouth of the cave with crowds of people cheering him on. Holding a heavy spear ready in both hands he lunged forward into the shadowed opening. He had not been seen since.

A little before noon on the following day, a young woman arrived. It was raining and there were no other villagers to see her approach, but she was smiling. Her name was Anja and she seemed to enjoy the raindrops. With only a little skip in her step she walked calmly into the darkness.

Once inside, challengers found that the dangers were fiercer than they had imagined. Weapons were useless against the foes in this place—they came from within. The first one to assail Stefan had been a dark cloud of his own Pride. He was still struggling with it a day later. The more courage he took from his rightness to succeed at this quest and rule over the village, the larger the monster he wrestled with became. He fought harder and it grew fiercer.

Anja was not able to see anyone else, but she was soon confronted by her own enemy. The first monster approached her, made of anger about things she could not control. It reached with tentacles and many hooks, ready to grasp and keep her, but she raised her arms and danced further into the cave, stepping easily to one side.

The next foe was her self-doubt, ready to breathe a gas that would weaken her limbs and leave her helpless on the floor. Anja twirled once, twice, smiling and spinning past.

Ahead of her, the beast of her life's misfortune waited hungrily. Nothing escaped its jaws. Those who tried to avoid it simply found themselves coming around the same corner again and again, sometimes tasting success elsewhere but always returning to hardship as well. It tempted Anja with promises of wealth and responsibility, ready to strike as soon as she was kept in place by the heavy prizes it offered.

Anja saw the piles of gold and medals on the stone floor but did not stop. She was not bound to the straight lines and competition that the other challengers assumed were the strongest way. Closing her eyes, the woman's smile grew bigger as she spread her *arms to feel the air move between her fingers. She sensed the stone surrounding the space, the air currents, the drip of water. She was in tune with nature and demanded nothing of it.*

The demon of her sorrow was one of the largest, and this she did not entirely avoid. It wailed that her being here was disastrous, that she should be afraid and mourn every event that had happened. She turned on one foot in front of it, her other held off the ground and moving in a slow circle. She had chosen not to engage with all the previous monsters but laid a hand on this one, acknowledging it. Her sorrow had helped make her who she was today, and while she did not choose to stay with it, she did not reject it either.

Moving past, steps still light, a smile on her face flowing from the depths of her heart, Anja left the other challengers to wrestle their heavy burdens while she entered the bright opening at the far end of the Cave.

The Dancer is very linked to cycles. Not only is this the shape of their physical movement, flowing around obstacles and moving to their own tempo, but it also reflects their experience in the world. The Dancer often finds themselves on streets they have previously walked but this time with a new understanding and making different choices.

When this card appears, it shows that we are all affected by cycles. We will be lucky and unlucky in our lives, and fate may bless us or deliver hardships. All we can do is survive these events as best we can.

Cycles move and return to the starting point and can indicate relief or trouble. Even if things are bad, we know that soon they will swing in the other direction and that nothing stays negative forever. Change always happens, and eventually some of that change will be good.

The problem with a motion that returns repeatedly to a start point is that the cycle also applies to behaviors we like less—to our habits, to choices we keep making which might not be the best ones for us. We're really good at repeating actions which feel nice but don't help us. While we stay locked in that pattern we won't move on to better places.

Luckily, the Dancer is an expert at navigating cycles. They can ride them safely or make a new path instead of staying within the current one. They have more awareness and self-knowledge than the Roles before the Hermit, have gone through wisdom and reconciliation, and no longer follow their old habits unless they choose to.

Fortune will always send varied things our way. We can study and recognise the cycle and decide how we will react to it—flowing with it painlessly or forging a new path. We can wait patiently until the right time to leave or use our knowledge to start preparing now.

NINE OF SPADES:
DANCER'S FOLLY
"MARA, LOST IN BEAUTY"

Illusion, Self-deception, Imbalance

The Queen of the Bay had ruled over the nearby villages since her arrival many years ago. Her name was Mara, and she pulled magic and enchantments from the water. Anyone who tried to stand up to her became lost in the web of illusions that she could bring forth.

One day, an old teacher walked up to the castle. He did not seem afraid but calmly made his way to the throne room where the queen was waiting. She had foretold his arrival and was prepared to overcome him with her spells.

"I am here to ask you to step aside and let the people rule themselves," he said to her. Mara laughed, and in a cruel but musical voice informed him that his life was at an end. She would daze him with magic and make him walk off the cliffs to fall into the sea.

Her first spell was one of fear, voices in a storm, chasing him and pleading with him. The teacher sat calmly, ignored the pleading calls, and looked intently through the suddenly black clouds to where the queen had previously sat. Eventually it became clear that he was not caught by this trap, so she released him from the vision.

The next one followed it immediately. Dreams of power and riches appeared on all sides of him, crowns and servants, glory and praise. He folded his arms and grunted impatiently. Soon she realized that he knew his own mind too well to fall for those tricks.

Finally, she prepared her most fearsome magic. From the sea mist she called up beautiful illusions. Jewels and works of art of such emotion and grace, animals playing together in peace, the sun and moon shining exquisitely down from the skies. In the heart of it lay her most reliable snare: an image of herself. This was a charm only a few had survived long enough to see, but all fell before it. Her face appeared as the most lovely that any could imagine, strong in its certainty, immortal in its purity in a way that her real features had never been. Mara's greed and cruelty always showed through in her real face, but not here.

This time, however, it was not enough. The teacher remained where he stood, arms folded, looking defiantly at all the fantastic creations. It was impossible! No mortal had resisted this before. How could they? She had sculpted the vision of her face to be the most captivating, admirable person who had ever lived. She had never even held the illusion for this length of time before. Looking at the perfect image before her now, she could see the impossible nobility of the cheekbones, the lustrous hair. Gazing into her own eyes, she lost sight of the other images—the slowly flowing waters, sparkle of sun on wet rocks, the beautiful bird calls. She could only see her creation.

Back in the castle, the old teacher watched as the Queen stood silently in the centre of the room, staring at nothing. She was captured by her own lies, as he knew she would be. One led by vanity and selfishness prized themselves above all others. The teacher had a home, a family, and friends to remind him to be humble and to keep his mind focused on what was really important. A mere illusionist had none of these things.

He walked away, and behind him the Queen stood enraptured by the beauty of her own making.

The Dancer is an extraordinary Role. Having learned all the previous lessons, they return to the world and see it entirely differently. They move through it in a new way, with wisdom and intuition. They open their senses to emotion and dance their way around problems, feeling the joy within. When you're that connected and avoiding most problems, there is a danger that you just want to close your eyes and lose yourself in the dance. Existing purely within intuition leads to a life full of wonder and sensitivity ... but it lacks balance. We can't passively move around all our challenges or tackle everything from just one viewpoint.

In particular, the Dancer sways with their eyes closed and listens to their own music. They avoid the common trap of believing that other people's opinions are more important than their own, certainly a valuable lesson (inner peace, control of your mind and joy are all good things to have instead of aggressive competition). But living this way also leads to being lost in sensation, avoiding responsibility, and only looking inward for every answer.

We don't live entirely in our inner world. Nearly all of us can benefit from bringing more of it into our daily actions, but we exist in the physical world too—and ignoring that fact can lead to problems. Going with the flow and finding an effortless path through the day needs a counterpart, a grounded and reliable heavy foundation that ensures our plans don't stay only in our heads.

This card suggests that we are falling for our own illusions. Listening to our own thoughts without asking other people for an opinion can make it very easy to lie to ourselves or invest in an outcome we want more. We can put people on a pedestal and see them as the perfect choice for us, when the reality is that they are only human as well. We can lose ourselves in sensation instead of concentrating on the outside world or believe that everyone thinks negative things about us when this isn't true.

A little illusion is good for anyone. Our intuition and emotions are extremely important, but make sure that this is not the only route you use to assess something. Get an outside opinion or look at evidence based in solid fact.

NINE OF HEARTS:
DANCER'S TRIUMPH
"HYUN-KI CHASES HIS MASTER"

Paths, Easy Progress, Harmony

"M-Master?"

All Hyun-Ki could see of the older figure was the familiar blue cap calmly making its way through the oncoming crowds. Trying to catch up, the student bumped into a tall man carrying a box of vegetables for market, who made a tutting noise. He tried to apologize, but the man was already gone and it seemed as through three more people had replaced him, all wanting to get past Hyun-Ki in the narrow street.

Why was his master going the wrong way, when it was nearly time for market? These roads were always chaotic at this time of day!

"Oh! Sorry, madam!"

Another member of the crowd gave him a look as he tried to back out of her way, only to push against someone else.

"I'm coming, master!"

Again the man in the blue cap calmly flowed along the street against the tide of people, slipping into gaps or sometimes taking a dignified step back to allow others to pass. Hyun-Ki was not finding it as easy, and was now out of breath and flustered, hoping that the hat would not get so far ahead of him that it would leave his sight.

It was infuriating! Every time he tried to gain speed, he bumped into someone's shoulder or had to leap back to avoid being knocked over entirely. The narrow street was so full of impatient people that their movement was like a rushing river, and he was foolish enough to be trying to swim against all the pressure coming the other way.

The anger was enough to make the panicked student finally remember the previous week's lesson, on moving like water. He decided that anything would be better than the exhausting struggle he was currently attempting, and so tried to imagine how to do that. A gap appeared in front of him, and he stepped into it. Then he found his way blocked by three people carrying boxes! Instead of trying to shoot forward and slip around them or back up hastily and worry at the progress his master was making ahead, Hyun-Ki let himself drift gently away from them. Soon, a space appeared to the right as the three drew level, and he was able to take it. Then the crowd moved with him for a moment, at a slower pace than he'd like, but he decided to match them and only change if the opportunity arose. It soon did, and he stepped forward and matched speed again. When oncoming merchants walked toward him, he gave way. When there was a space, he slid into it. He was no longer out of breath and was moving a surprising distance.

Suddenly Hyun-Ki realized that the figure in front of him was his master, smiling gently. "Good. You stopped resisting.

When someone tried to push you back, you flowed around them,
like water. Not against them, straining your muscles and damag-
ing you both."

"Now, turn around and go to the market, we need food for
dinner."

The Dancer finds themselves moving along the same streets
as the Noble but with a totally different approach. Time
away as the Hermit has taught the Dancer what is really
important in life—and it is not possessions or competition.
They move happily while listening to inner music and wait
for life to flow the way they require before stepping into the
current.

We are taught to strive, achieve, and work hard along
the normal routes: to look attractive (according to whatever our country and time period says that is right now) and
to value certain things above others. Some of the choices
society suggests for these are extremely negative and will
cause distress to anyone who tries to pursue or apply all of
them. There are other ways to live.

The Dancer's Triumph is that making these new choices
will open a path that wasn't there before. Sidestepping the
hazards and moving away from the crowded road that everyone else is using gets you to your destination by faster and
more scenic routes. Moving with your own tide instead of
against it will let you swim farther before you are tired, while

fighting it will only leave you in the same place you were, exhausted and angry.

This idea of not fighting a tide absolutely does not mean that you don't fight against injustice or avoid anything that takes effort. The Dancer has self-knowledge from their time as the Hermit and is relaxed and happy enough to let the love in their heart influence their decisions. They do not abandon others or back down from resisting people who do wrong, they simply find an efficient and natural way to progress which takes less energy. The Dancer dances forward, around, behind. If an enemy attacks, the Dancer is not there. If an opportunity appears, the Dancer glides into it.

This card represents a new path opening up due to your actions coming from a place of wisdom more so than in your past. It is easy to follow, because the Dancer's attitude makes everything easy. If there is a brick wall ahead, do not strain and angrily try to push it down—skip around it. The Triumph is in being able to walk with only peace and joy driving you, and to find the experience easier and more meaningful than before, ignoring obstacles and holding to what is really important. The result of living this way is that you reach your destination faster, with less stress or conflict. This very quickly leads to new opportunities as you arrive safe and refreshed at your destination ahead of the crowd.

THE TENS: THE MAGICIAN

The Magician balances all the previous Roles. They have learnt the wisdom of each and can wield it in the right amounts. They have also learnt when to stay still and silent, and that sometimes taking action is not the best answer.

The Magician is a Role which is always reaching in several directions. Whether it is to create a balance, juggle many moving forces or find their true nature, they deal with multiple aspects and know the best way to use each. They do not start a new task until they have a solid foundation, but also do not let themselves be slowed by burdens if a burst of determined energy could help things along.

The Magician is the final Role on the Magician's Journey and represents a place of success. From the single-minded Hunter, through the challenges of society and our own emotions, the Roles expand our knowledge until we are ready to control the world with courage, love, endurance, and a quick mind. They allow us to dive into life without being held back, be true to ourselves and make the choices which will lead to us being truly happy. They leave us with inner peace as well as the energy needed to make change. We have compassion for others but also secure boundaries.

The Magician knows themselves and knows how to walk in the world without fear, encounter change without stress, and guide those around them with wisdom. They are strong enough to be kind. They have achieved balance and mastery.

TEN OF CLUBS:
MAGICIAN'S PROMISE
"JESS THROWS AN ACORN"

Balance, Self-Discipline, Fairness

Izarre walked alongside Jess and asked excitedly: "Will you call the animals for me? And sing the rain away, and make the tree give me a shiny apple?"

Jess—slightly taller and recently graduated as a name-speaker—simply smiled and shook her head. Izarre didn't give up. "What if we went to the stream, and you made it spout and sway like a fountain?"

Pausing at the gate, her answer was not what the excitable one had hoped for.

"Do you know the price for working magic? What it means to bend things out of their natural rhythms, and what must be done to achieve it?"

"Well ... no. That's why you went to school and I didn't."

Searching on the ground, Jess picked up an acorn. "See this? I can throw it." She did, and it sailed through the air. "That's fair. I found it, I spent the energy to throw it, I moved my arm. Using magic is different. If I used magic to move the acorn, I'm asking it to fly over there without tiring my muscles. I have to get the energy from somewhere else instead."

"And that leaves the other place without the energy?"

"Yes, but that's only a tiny part of it. The bigger problem is how to justify doing it at all." She stopped Izarre from interrupting again with a stern look and continued: "The acorn should be on the ground. It had a destiny there. I just picked it up and made a choice about it. Maybe now it won't take root in the new place it landed. Maybe someone will slip on it. When I decided to change its fate, the stars listened. When it hit the ground, the rocks and soil trembled. Each action we take, big or small, has consequences. So it's not just how to balance the forces I would use to magically throw the acorn so that I don't accidentally create a desert where a lush valley was. It's whether the world needed the acorn to be in its original place, and what right I had to move it."

Izarre looked disappointed but took Jess's hand and kissed it. "I understand."

A small smile perked the taller one's lips, and she made a flowing motion with the other hand, producing a green apple from the air. At the astonished look from her companion, she shrugged.

"Eh. The balance isn't that delicate. The world won't miss one apple, when it creates such beautiful joy on your face in exchange."

Balance is a rare gift which becomes important to all of us at different times. Like this card, it is a Promise. If anything is worse than usual now, balance promises that it will one day return to normal.

The Magician Role spends a lot of time thinking about balance. The Magician's Gambit card is one of frantic motion, but this Promise is calm instead. Promise cards often deal with the idea of a perfect destination, not the messy reality of needing to juggle events right now. When looking to this one for guidance, it is usually an assurance that balance will come. Acting to bring it about is more the job of the Gambit card, this Promise needs less intervention on your part.

What could "balance" mean? It could refer to the inner balance of your mind, the amounts of work and play in your life, or how often you get to see those you love. It doesn't have to be equal and still on all sides—you might need a lot of a certain thing to happen, and keep happening. As long as the requirements on the other end of the scale are also met, this situation can continue for a long time. One end can be larger than the other if you keep putting the energy in to hold it there. This isn't automatically a boring card; it can promise more than just a flat, level field.

The Magician has learned many lessons to reach this place: that the attractive prizes of glory or temporary power in the outside world are false without inner mastery, that one rule does not apply to every situation but instead we must use all the tools we have to choose the best outcome each time. Now they must reach into several different areas and invest in them all to create the best kind of balanced change.

You can only do this if you concentrate on the same aspects as the Magician does. Make sure you have solid foundations and security, that your mind is clear and sharp, that your emotions are under control and ready to be explored, and that you have the passion and will to make the necessary changes happen. This card is a prompt to think about all those things and be ready to act later.

TEN OF DIAMONDS
MAGICIAN'S GAMBIT
"ISLA AND THE FOUR SPIRITS"

Juggling, Reducing Chaos, Applying Knowledge

Isla entered the chamber and could immediately see that the Wise Woman had been correct. Everything was dangerously out of place. The ceiling was lost in smoke, and the windows were obscured. Gathering her wits, Isla began the work.

On her left, the spirit of Fire had nearly gone out. The Magician called to it, reminding it of the courage, passion, and hunger that drove fire to charge forth in search of new action. How could it be sleeping when such a crisis was upon the tower? She took the fine woods from a rack nearby and fed them to the flames. Slowly, the embers bloomed to light and the spirit resumed its normal strength, eager and determined.

Over in the other corner, the spirit of Water rested in silence. Its still and dark depths were unmoving. Isla sang a song of love, of clear bright waters rushing in a stream under the sunlight, of mysterious currents flowing around any enemy who tried to stop them with order or rules. A bubble emerged in the centre of the pool, and then another. The murkiness retreated, replaced by a bright and pure flow of sweet water.

The spirit of Air was frantic. Speaking to it, reasoning with its logic and long sight, the Magician reminded the Air of open mountains, gusts that travelled into valleys and played around the caves and trees with nothing to block their quick thought. There was no call to emotion or passion here, only communication and sharp insight. Seeing the recovery of the Fire and Water, the Air spirit calmed and resumed darting around the ceiling in its normal manner.

Then Isla turned to the spirit of Earth, the cascade of rock and soil that took up the far end of the room. This would be the most difficult. When the spirits had lost their balance, the Earth had reached for its greatest defense—solid, unmoving stone. Patient and tough, it could not be talked out from behind the unbreakable walls. With enough time, it felt, all things would return to comfortable normality.

But Isla had to try, and quickly. Without Earth's stabilizing influence, the other elements were running too loosely. Fire and Air together were exploring with more speed, Water was without boundaries. Most importantly, the tree growing in the centre of the chamber urgently needed the return of light from the windows, something that would not be possible until the Earth spirit was part of the balance. Isla spoke to the Earth of the other side of its nature, which was not the patient mountain but instead the life of green shoots and buds, the great creative energy within the soil. Slowly she coaxed it out from immobile stone to warm mud, in search of sunlight and the soft kiss of rain.

As the spirits of the Elements reassured each other, calm was restored. The air cleared, and the boundaries of the room could once again be seen. On the right and left, ornate windows let in their promised light—one side golden and one silver. With the elements in harmony, the sun and moon shone their blessed rays upon the tree in the centre and the Magician stood before their work, holding the balance.

The Magician's Gambit is to juggle the many forces of the World, using all the Magician has learned. This is not the gentle inner balance the Magician's Promise assures us of but a messy, constantly moving situation. It is the task of navigating the many challenges of life.

To succeed, the Magician must look very carefully at what surrounds them and then act. This is a card of action guided by wisdom. As with all Gambit cards, it is a challenge that can be failed, but reassures us "You know enough to do this. You can keep all these juggled balls in the air and still have a peaceful mind."

Though the Warrior teaches the first steps in taking action, the Magician does it slightly differently. Balance can require transformation, the conversion of multiple forces around you at the same time. The Healer advises us to do this with compassion, the Hermit with a calm mind. The Dancer would be very good at doing so, if they weren't so caught up in sinking into their own intuition as much as possible. The move from there to the Magician is one of taking responsibility and staying grounded.

In readings, this card tells us to get ready to juggle! There will be more than one issue that needs dealing with, and we'll have to do some work. It also tells us that we *do* have the skills to manage it. The Magician is the most advanced Role—they have the expertise to make a success of the most difficult situations. They recognise that each issue has multiple parts and therefore reject simple single answers.

This card may have a lot of movement in it, so the person the reading is about would need to come to the situation with energy and confidence in order to stay juggling.

TEN OF SPADES:
MAGICIAN'S FOLLY
"MOTHER OLIVIA'S MAGIC"

Simple Tasks, Avoiding Arrogance, Routine Work

Mother Olivia was the greatest magician in the world. She had travelled to the ends of every land and beyond, where she had gathered many powers. Now she lived quietly in the village of Elsom. One autumn day, the fishermen needed wind for their sails, so she untied the smallest knot on a string. She had used it to catch the great wind Varlatha, high on the slopes of the mountain of Hjek, and now called on the tiniest fraction of that fearsome gale's strength. The boats were soon back at shore.

That winter was harsh, and the villagers gathered in the great hall for warmth. When the wooden logs in the fireplace would not light, she pulled a gleam from the red ruby eye of the dread monster Sissarnat, which she had fought and defeated in the vast desert of Paraf. That monster had been able to blast a man to ash with only a gaze. She aimed its destruction towards the fireplace and the logs lit merrily.

When the spring came and the shoots needed rain, Olivia opened the tiniest corner of a cloth bag that contained the legendary storm clouds of Rilga, caught far out into the waters of the

Isles of Brac. She had learned the trick after besting the Sage of Gonric in a contest of riddles at his crystal castle home.

In the warm summer, enemies appeared on the border of their lands. She frightened them away with the echo of a shriek from the banshee of the caves of Rolthen, which had dwelled at the end of a maze of dark stone. She had woven its deadly cry into a skein of wool, and now unpicked just the few threads it would take to cause an army to flee but not kill them.

Later that year, the chief of the Magician's Guild visited the village. She saw the children fed and happy, the buildings secure the community giving love to each other and their neighbors. She did not ask to see a demonstration of Mother Olivia's power. She knew immediately that Olivia was worthy to lead the Guild and asked her to do so.

The Magician has grown in skill as they've progressed through the Roles but that does not mean that they should only ever deal with complicated or magical things now. The Folly of those who are accomplished is to think that they live in a special place where they don't need to do basic tasks anymore. (This is especially true of magicians.)

One of the most powerful actions we can take is do a really good job at something we're an expert at. This can be completing a simple action brilliantly, or helping others who are just starting out. This card says to simplify a situation down to something you know that you can easily achieve—and not to want the situation to be more difficult than that.

There are other benefits to the idea of going back to basics: the Magician avoids arrogance and bad habits if they follow it. We're all still human, even when pride makes us think we've earned the right not to get involved with the kind of tasks we used to like less. When we're lost in the storm of juggling complex forces, we need to remember that simplicity also works.

The Magician's Journey is almost over. They have learned wisdom, experienced responsibility and power, worked out which causes they will stand for and gained the skill they need to balance the demands of life. This is the final Folly— that they think everything must always be so busy, perfectly handled, or filled with only complex issues. They think they have nothing left to learn. This is never true for anyone! Simplify, and stay humble.

TEN OF HEARTS:
MAGICIAN'S TRIUMPH
"ALANNA FACES THE DRAGON"

Mastery, Completion, Success Through Learning

Alanna stepped calmly to the edge of the shore and looked out at the glittering, gentle waters. The sunset turned the sands around her into a warm shade of orange as small waves lapped at her feet.

She called the Dragon.

The waters parted with a crash as the massive scaled head of the beast rose from the sea and regarded the small figure before it.

"You must be a mage, to call me from my depths."

"I have come to the end of my studies. I wanted to talk."

"I do not talk with mages. I judge them, and they destroy themselves."

"Judge me then, old one."

The Dragon began its assault, reaching into Alanna's heart and bringing forth all the pain and difficulty it could. The fears which stopped her taking action. The hurt of previous losses, and knowledge that loved ones could not be protected from all ills in the future. How she controlled herself when violence occurred. How she had opened her defenses to another, and been abandoned, and done it again anyway. How much she contributed to the suffering of animals, humans, and the fertile earth. How she had sat with her books and learned over years. The times when she had not met the expectations of her teachers, and whether that meant she was a failure as a person. The panic of self-image when someone excelled in a way that she couldn't. Those times when she had chosen to demand the respect that she had earned instead of taking second place as others automatically expected her to do. The times she had been tempted by popularity but not abused it. Her love of the trees and stars, and sorrow that the day would come when she could not see them again. Her ability to find happiness in normal moments. Her wondering whether anything made a difference, when the dark shores of death awaited everyone. Her caring for others. The peace she made with her enemies. The daring she showed when the world required changing. Her fierce love for life and all the good things in existence.

When the Dragon did this to a Mage, it was always the same. Some part of them would reach out from the inside and make the Mage react with fear, hate, and violence against everything they saw as threats. They would claw at themselves, and either die or walk the rest of their days with unbalanced pain in their limbs.

This did not happen.

The Dragon spoke again.

"The elements are united within you. You can act or stay silent. You are not ruled by fear. You are not numbed to love. You have mastered this life. You know who you are."

"And now," Alanna called to the ancient power before her, "I want to learn more."

This is the final card of the Magician's Journey and it represents completion and mastery. The Court cards after this section are different; they deal with large and eternal outside forces, instead of daily matters or personal growth. Magician's Triumph is the final card of the main cycle and the ultimate destination.

Any situation you are asking about will be a safe and complete success. You have the skills to win, and everything up to that point will combine to move to a natural and glorious end. It symbolizes all the lessons of every card in this book so far across all ten Roles.

Frequently, what this card refers to in your real life is success through skill, even at very difficult tasks. If you're going up against an expert, you can beat that expert. You move forwards in strength and have every advantage. If a question is about timing, the action is happening now, but the indication is that the larger situation will also come to an end (in the way you intend) soon.

What this card means internally is more complex. The Magician knows their true nature, feels in control, and can make changes happen while being in a good, secure, peaceful place mentally. However, this is a Triumph—the ultimate Triumph. The background noise of this card is trumpets and fanfare with high energy. So while the Magician has learned everything they need to, this is still a very active and powerful card and not one of quiet endings.

If you need to take action, this card says to make it a wise one. See the whole picture and act decisively to bring events to a successful end. Make sure that your decisions are informed by looking back over the whole history and are worthy of someone who can achieve mastery.

Magician's Triumph is always welcome in a reading because of the sheer power of positive outcomes it brings. You can do the task, events will go your way triumphantly, and the movie's end credits will roll on a celebration of success.

CHAPTER FOUR

THE COURT CARDS

The meanings of the Court cards in this deck are very different from the numbers and Aces. The concepts the Court cards bring to a reading are often events which happen to us from outside rather than something we can control or improve within ourselves. We are not these figures, they are external to us (and eternal). They are powerful forces with their own history and personalities. For example, the Queen brings luck of a type that is either random, good or bad. We cannot train ourselves in "good luck," it is only something we can encounter, or make room for and hope that it appears more often in our lives.

Modern Court card designs started in a form made by Pierre Marechal in Rouen, France, around 1565. They were quite different from the modern images: as mentioned earlier, the court figures had legs! Their clothes, hands, and weapons have all changed over the centuries as well. The double-headed versions we use now were introduced in the mid-1800s.

If you can find a deck that replicates the older designs, they are often both beautiful and very powerful when used in divination. They can still be found in English decks from the 1700s and even American poker decks from the mid-1800s. Replicas of these and lots of other styles are available to buy today quite cheaply and are fantastic cards to use in divination.

THE JACKS: THE TRICKSTER

In most playing card divination systems, a Jack represents a carefree young man who cannot be trusted. Anything a Jack (or a Trickster) promises you is a lie. This doesn't have to be a bad thing, however! Jacks are exciting—they do the unexpected by an unconventional route. They don't put on work clothes and steadily apply themselves to a predictable profession; instead, they seek new answers and confront the scarier questions within.

All Magicians are also Tricksters. Trickery is built into many shamanic practices, and even into the toolset of people who would be teachers. After all, the Trickster knows something you don't—they will reveal something surprising or act in a way you don't expect. There are many positive examples of how you can learn from someone who does that.

Although the illustration of a Jack in modern cards is male, Tricksters come in all forms. Some Jacks are Jennys, and some (again particularly in certain shamanic traditions) are a third or nonbinary gender. The spirit of Jacks in the modern deck of cards is also varied. With the Court cards, we encounter pictures that spark imagination and associations all over the world—from the poker tables of Vegas and the legends of the Old West to anywhere a hand of cards is dealt in fun. Jacks appear in all of them, sometimes winking at us.

JACK OF CLUBS:
TRICKSTER'S PROMISE
"SABINA BETRAYED"

Lies, Betrayal, Worthless Assurances

Lady Sabina sat across the table from her opponent and studied the cards in her hand again. A good score, but not certain to win. She smiled to her enemy and the crowd of people who stood behind him in the small room. Her own loyal courtiers were similarly huddled behind her.

She continued to smile as she caught the eye of the servant who had managed to join the enemy's household recently. Long months it had taken, and much deception, but now he was placed in the group of figures directly behind Lord Gunter and able to see his cards. Able to signal to her when to bet, and when to fold.

Such a beautiful boy. And so eager to please her. With his help in this final game, Sabina's victory would be complete and her status in society assured.

Lord Gunter raised a huge amount. There was a gasp from the room. The servant was biting his lip slightly—wait, was that right? That was their signal! She checked his face again and there could be no doubt. He bit his lip and nodded to her, slowly.

Excitement warmed her. This meant Gunter's bet was a bluff —he was holding nothing of value and she would crush him! With a last look and a nod from the boy, she put her entire fortune into play.

More gasps from the room, and a clamor of barely hushed disbelief.

Lord Gunter turned his cards, and Sabina felt a shock run through her whole body. Kings! What? This was impossible, the boy would never have—she looked up to find the face of her spy in the crowd once more, and saw him staring directly at her with a slow smile. This wasn't right! Beside him, a girl—she knew that one. That was the servant girl she'd had whipped and banished from the house last year.

All the money on the table was taken away. She had nothing.

Across the room, Vihan and Jiya held hands tightly and savored the panicked expression on the face of their tormentor. Long months of deception had been worth it. They were together now, and rich, and she was ruined. All those nights of risk, so that she would believe one lie.

A "Trickster's Promise" is a lie. Because the Court cards always represent forces outside you, this lie comes from someone else. It is a Promise that cannot be relied upon, the classic trapdoor that opens beneath you when you thought the ground was safe.

The Court cards tend to modify other results more than they tell a story of their own. So while Trickster's Promise in isolation can mean a lie or a deceitful person, in combination with another card it tell us that the message from the other is the lie. For example, Noble's Gambit means friendship and loyalty—but combined with Trickster's Promise the message becomes "This friendship is false." It renders other positive cards worthless and shows their statements are unreliable.

This all sounds very negative and it certainly can be. The Trickster is a figure who (by definition) catches people by surprise in ways they don't want. However, it can also be positive. Sometimes we need someone to shake things up, to topple a situation we thought was locked down and unchangeable, to turn the tables on those who usually win.

Tricksters deceive for many reasons, but some of those reasons can be honorable. Shamans and teachers are often Tricksters, as well as anyone who does stage magic tricks with cards. The trick itself has no good or evil to it; it is the intent and outcome which decide the value. Who is being deceived, and why?

Historically, Jacks are tricky characters. They are bold, young men who are unreliable and like themselves too much. They can be effective, but there are always others above them in power. In response, they tend to resort to routes that aren't a straight confrontation (which they would notably lose).

This card does the opposite of typical Promise cards. They show the idealized version of a Role, the perfect imagined best outcome which could await us in the future. But this one doesn't have any future—it's a betrayal that is happening right now. If you receive Trickster's Promise in a one-card reading, it's a warning. There is a trick or lie coming that you're probably not expecting.

If you are performing a reading with more than one card, look at any others joined to this Jack, because their meanings could be reversed or unreliable. If Trickster's Promise appears in a place that suggests it as an action you should take, then be like the Trickster—don't play by the rules. Hold onto that rebellious spirit and know that your own individual choices can be better than following strict laws.

JACK OF DIAMONDS: TRICKSTER'S GAMBIT
"BETH MEETS A GOOD DOG"

Unexpected Lessons, Risks for Large Gains

Beth sighed and contemplated the suitors. A miller. Some minor noble who loved himself more than he ever would her. The head of the countinghouse—oh good, she could write numbers in books for the rest of her days.

Her father's guards stood stiffly by the door. There was no escaping this fate; she would have to choose. At least if she complied with her father's wishes, it would mean a comfortable life. A comfortable, boring life.

One of the guards yawned just as the decorative window next to them opened, and a large brown dog bounded in. Henry was a good dog. He knew this. He was also very enthusiastic about making new friends but couldn't stop jumping up at everyone long enough to really get it right, so they always seemed angry with him. He tried anyway.

As soon as the guards were busy with Henry, the window next to Beth also opened. On the other side was the gardener's boy, Petar, holding out his hand to pull her through.

"Ryn sent me! Come with me now, and she'll meet you tonight."

"Ryn? I can't! I'd lose everything!"

"Your choice, but you have to go now." At the far end of the room the guards were still shouting at Henry the very good dog, who was leaping at each of them and having a great time.

Beth knew she only had moments. She looked at her father's hall, and then at the grubby hand which was waiting to help her to a new—but uncertain—life. She took another breath and decided.

A Gambit shows a Role doing work according to that Role's nature hoping for the best outcome. The Trickster's Gambit is to take the unconventional wisdom that only the Trickster has and make a difference with it. In this case, the Trickster is not you, as all the Court cards are external forces. This gamble is being made by someone else. But what could a Trickster's gamble look like?

The perhaps unexpected answer is that it can be a positive lesson: unexpected wisdom or help from others in a way that surprises you. Tricksters have access to knowledge or instincts which others don't (they have to, or they could never trick anyone). Many do what they do for money, or bad intentions, but some do it to try and change the minds of the average crowd. They have an enormous amount of self-belief: while everyone else follows the road from A to

B to C, Tricksters want to show you a really great shortcut from Z to M. This Gambit can be someone trying to teach you a lesson in an unconventional way, so you should listen.

The other definition for this card can be a Trickster taking a risk, particularly in gambling. They have a con going on, and it's the moment when it succeeds or fails. That action might not be deceitful, it is just a gamble by someone who does not take the conventional route.

The "lesson" meaning is usually a positive one. Someone will show you wisdom from an angle you're not expecting. This is a great opportunity! We can all learn from other people, no matter how old or experienced we become. The Trickster is not you, so the trick is not from your own hidden knowledge. Perhaps you have been wrong, and now it is time to look at the situation again and forget your old assumptions. Once you have discovered the unusual wisdom, it could give you an advantage that others don't know about.

The other meaning is less welcomed and needs to be studied carefully. Someone who is not you has a plan in motion, and there's a trick to it. This Gambit is not straightforward, like the Smith making an item and succeeding on the strength of hard work. This one is instead a very, very fragile situation that depends on a lot of luck.

We also have a clue for what the end result could be. A Trickster making their play at the card table is not doing it for a small prize. Trickery involves taking the shortcut, going for the jackpot. (The word "jackpot" comes from a type of Poker invented in the late 1800s where the money grew until someone could start the game with a hand containing two Jacks or better.) It suggests a big reward which you find the fast and risky route to get to, not the slow and boring way.

Both definitions come to the same conclusion: we should keep watch for unexpected opportunities, and take advantage of them if they appear instead of rejecting them because they look unusual. Tricksters (much like street magicians, clowns, some holy figures) can be aggravating or annoying to us, deliberately. We don't like surprises, and a Trickster is nothing without surprise. Be brave and reach for the new events if you can. Seek out those who can teach you lessons and listen for wisdom from unexpected places. Prepare for a situation where a lot of risky, quick moves are in progress.

JACK OF SPADES:
TRICKSTER'S FOLLY
"HARRY'S RUN CUT SHORT"

Honesty, Justice, Exposing Liars

Harry was in a good mood. The last town hadn't had any real prizes for him to take, only the little he'd managed to trick and steal from its elderly and desperate inhabitants. There was some sneaking into houses, some cheating at cards. It had been too small a place to safely operate in for any length of time, and as a stranger he was under suspicion when people's savings went missing, so he'd moved on. Today's location was much better! A trade route meant rich merchants spending their money here, and he was already surrounded by busy figures in fine clothing walking up and down the street.

He'd also met Pia the night before, a young woman who had just arrived from far across the land. She would be today's job.

When he reached her room, Pia smiled and let him in. The golden bracelet she'd worn previously wasn't on her wrist now, but Harry wasn't worried. She had money and it would soon be his. He turned to shut the door and was surprised to see a large man standing by the wall, already closing it. From the far corner, another man appeared. Everyone was armed.

Harry looked to Pia. "Darling? I don't know wh—"

She held up a badge and announced that she was with the militia. Oh well, it seemed his victims in the previous towns had wanted justice. But this wasn't too bad yet. He could still talk his way out of it ... or try the window!

The man behind the door moved to block the window.

"Pia, I'm sure this is a misunderstanding ..."

"No mistake. You are Harold Brown, wanted in several towns to the east for stealing and worse. I'm arresting you."

He looked around one last time, in case any of the others were the sort who might free him for a bribe. Their faces said no.

Harry had wriggled out of many situations, but today the forces of order would not be denied. He sighed as the cuffs clamped tightly around his wrists.

After the definite lie that is the Trickster's Promise and the gamble without doing the hard work that is the Gambit, it is nice to know that at least one of the Trickster's outcomes is more honest. The Folly of the Trickster is pushing their luck too far and getting caught.

When this Folly is seen in a reading the forces of order will win, shortcuts will fail, and justice will be served. People will play fair, and those who have been deceitful will be seen for the honorless folk they are.

This honesty is especially powerful in combination with other cards. It says that the other is true—for example,

Lover's Promise is an idealized fantasy of how good things could be with another person, but paired with this card the message is that you can trust it. Anyone who acted deceitfully against the best outcome would be found out, and no unexpected tricks are coming along soon.

Justice such as this sounds great, but it can still be challenging. After all, justice is not only receiving a fair result when you are wronged, but also getting what you deserve when you have wronged another, which can be less welcome. We all lie a little bit. It might be in how we deliberately appear to others or the small things we pretend to agree with because it's easier to get along with people. How many actions in your life do you only take for appearances? What happens when the real you must step up and be seen? A Trickster has a hidden self, just as we do, and often the aspects that we hide from the outside world are actually our most genuine parts. A card that exposes Tricksters should make everyone pause.

The easy way to deal with this card is to make sure that you have been compassionate like the Healer. Examine the situation without emotion, like the Hermit. There will be no tricks allowed in this reading—this card will ensure that any attempts will be noticed. That keen observation is a gift to us because it gives us certainty even when other cards might include the risks of Gambits. The reverse of that gift is that we also need to be honest with ourselves.

Don't lie, because you can't fake this. Don't hide behind deceptions. Look inside. Look carefully at the lies you want to hear or the appearance you wear for convenience. The Court cards are external forces, so you are not the Trickster in this scenario, but make sure that you are not caught along with them when the spotlight of truth shines on the situation.

JACK OF HEARTS:
TRICKSTER'S TRIUMPH
"LEO PLAYS IN THE WOODS"

Jackpot, Great Assistance, Unconventional Routes

Dead leaves crunched under Leo's feet as he made his way into the forest. The trees were twisted and there were few clearings, but eventually he found the one who he sought. The Old Man of the Woods sat there on the ground, his long hood down over his face.

"Why do you come?"

The youth answered with a wide smile. "I hear you have cards! I would wager my life against them."

The hooded figure did not move from his space, so Leo walked over and sat in front of him.

"If I deal from the deck, it cannot be undone."

"I know. I make the bet anyway."

With a sigh, the Old Man reached into his robe and produced a ragged pack of cards. They were yellow with age and had strange pictures in faded ink. His voice didn't change.

"Choose a number."

Leo nodded, and said "Three."

"Very well."

The first card was laid on the ground. It showed a figure killed by many spears and arrows.

"Oh, that doesn't look too good! I'm glad I didn't choose that, then."

Wordlessly, the Old Man turned another card from the pack and laid it on the dry dirt floor of the clearing. This one showed a figure crushed under rocks.

"Well, that isn't exactly hopeful either! Do you get many disappointed customers, wizened one?"

The Old Man did not move his head, but the voice emerged from the hood again.

"I have the power to grant whatever the cards say. It was decided that those seeking a fast route to glory or riches are unvirtuous and should be punished. Therefore all the cards lead only to death and ruin." He put his hand onto the next card of the pack. "This one will set your fate."

The boy's grin didn't change. "I must say, the rumors suggested all kinds of good things. But now I learn that I am doomed. Oh dear."

The card was turned and placed on the ground, but the Old Man jerked back in surprise. This was not like the others. It had the same ragged faded paper, but the image shown on it was of a young, handsome man, wearing royal clothes and carrying a bag of coins. He had a big smile, which matched the smile currently on the face of the youth. Their hair even looked the same.

The Old Man stared at it.

"How did you ... that is not one of my cards."

"But you must do its bidding!" said the younger with a wink.

"Yes."

And so Leo, now Lord Leon, returned to town to take charge of his new castle and begin a long life of luxury and enjoyment.

The Jack of Hearts in many systems is untrustworthy: a handsome young man with a wink and smile who absolutely cannot be depended on. Here, the Triumph carries so much success with it that the outcome is only positive.

Success for a Trickster is about taking a shortcut to win the whole Jackpot. By definition, they don't want to do all the hard work to get there the slow way, they use an alternative (and usually surprising) route to win everything in one go.

The Court cards in this system do not represent you. They are large, powerful forces that affect you from outside, and the Trickster is one of the most established. Tricksters (and indeed cheeky young men named Jack) have a very long history. When they appear in a reading, they usually modify any other card they relate to; in this case, the meaning is great success without having to pay the cost.

The help this card speaks of often comes to you from others but can also refer to circumstances that make something previously unlikely more possible for you. One specific example of how this Triumph often works is that some knowledge or belief you have (where you disagree with the traditional way of doing things) turns out to be the key to progress and leads to a great outcome. You should embrace this alternative way of doing things.

Others will see that the unusual approach has paid off. Taking the shortcut makes all kinds of successes possible. Using a trick, a student can beat a master. A teacher can show their class a new way of thinking, unrelated to the basic concepts they are expected to build from. Concepts which are dismissed as wrong by society will succeed anyway.

This is a card of unconventional routes and doing things the easy way. If you asked a question on how to approach a problem, the answer is the opposite of "do all the hard work." Trust your luck and any exciting ideas.

THE QUEENS: THE LADY

The Queen is Lady Luck. She has a place in every deck, and in every room where cards are dealt.

The Lady is very different from the Trickster. The Trickster acts, they have a plan, they represent all those in the world who refuse to accept the conventional routes to achievement. By contrast, the Lady is pure chance. In three of her cards she is variations of luck, and in one, the promise of what could happen if your luck is the best. She is much more of an abstract force.

The Lady has been part of playing cards since long before the Queens gained their current images. Everyone who is drawn to games and gambling, everyone who rolls the dice or plays a hand is aware of the Lady. She can be a friend ... or not. Either way, she walks through the deck and every reading.

QUEEN OF CLUBS:
LADY'S PROMISE
"AGNETHA AND THE FIREFLY"

Temptation, Excitement, Future Possibilities

Agnetha was an old woman now. Her days of reigning as the leader of her country had been satisfying, at first. Money and power, the respect of her people, even travel and new sights had been available to her. She had visited foreign lands and spoken with scholars, eaten the finest foods, listened to majestic music.

Now she stood in the House of Chance and despaired. This noisy room was full of people playing dice or cards, and planning races. Just as with everything else recently even their feverish excitement could not make her feel any response at all. She had seen it before and now her mind and body only felt dull. Agnetha stood silently watching the tables and players.

As she waited in one spot, unmoving and bored, the spirit of the House came down to speak to her. It appeared in the form of a royal adviser, standing just behind her shoulder and speaking softly into her ear.

"Don't you find the activities fascinating?"

"No. Money does not interest me, nor meaningless games. The world is known. This room holds nothing new."

"Oh, but you are wrong. So very wrong. Look at the card table over there. Each card brings new stories. Who can guess what will happen? Maybe a peasant will be made a King. Maybe all the cards numbered eight will be drawn in the same round, even when the self-proclaimed expert over there in the hat assumed it couldn't happen, and he bet money that he doesn't have."

"Do you think that I should be interested in the misfortunes of gamblers?"

"No! In the infinite play of Chance! When the bets are in and the cards are down, there is one hot moment of possibility where the universe holds its breath. A suspended point in reality. In that time, anything can be true. Anything can be created. It could be a resounding triumph, or a small loss. A romance and life of luxury, or sweet revenge."

The spirit moved around to stand behind her other ear, while Agnetha remained staring straight ahead. It continued:

"All things could be created, any story told ... but only if you keep playing. Just one more round. Creating new, truly unknown outcomes. New adventures. New legends. But you have to play again."

And slowly, the Queen felt the pull of it. The warm, firefly glow of exciting possibility. She thought she had seen all that these lands had to offer, but in the silent undecided space before the dice fell to the table there existed everything that could be. She watched some cards. They were dealt from the deck ... now the outcome was fixed, a win for the woman in blue. More—

a new round, and again the tempting firefly pull of nothing being decided... until it was. She stepped forwards, needing it again. She knew that it was only cards, only dice, but if she could just have another round then she could return to that magical place where possibilities opened. Where she could feel inspired and excited, long after she'd thought that was lost to her.

The spirit withdrew, satisfied.

The other three cards of the Lady in this deck are themed around Luck, but this one isn't. This is a calling, a beckoning to something that genuinely could work out well for you. It is the allure of possibilities, but it is also her Promise. The Lady looks after her people and will ensure that you win enough for the temptation to continue. This is therefore actually a card of minor good luck, not just neutral wishing.

Primarily though, the meaning of this card is "temptation." When Chance is available then anything can happen—including good outcomes. This means that a wanted prize can always be just a few seconds away. In readings this optimism is added to any cards affected by this one, and the situation becomes more tempting.

Although these temptations usually have a good reason (you actually could gain a lot from winning) the need to gamble is rarely something you want in your life. Divination is, in a way, the opposite of gambling. It attempts to find the truth and ask questions instead of risking everything on unknown answers. Look very carefully at the situation that this card is advising you to jump into and ensure that it's in your interests.

If you can be sure that it's safe to indulge in the temptation, then things get exciting. People are drawn to the hope and possibilities that the Lady promises because those prizes are real. In many situations, future possibilities themselves can be the goal, opening up change where there wasn't one before.

This is an emotional card. It isn't about counting numbers, and it doesn't say that you can gain anything by working carefully. It calls to our emotions and promises fun and beauty, and those are always worth considering. Look to the future with excitement but check that any temptation on offer isn't just empty or foolish.

QUEEN OF DIAMONDS:
LADY'S GAMBIT
"FRANCOIS FLIPS A COIN"

Pure Chance

The Lady wandered through the worlds. She examined the furious heart of burning stars and decided the ways in which their pieces would break apart.

She swept down to the hot water pools at the base of a mountain where animals bathed, and parted the mists with her intention, playing in the heat and cold.

She saw a trader climb down from his horse to examine the frayed foot-strap he leant all his weight upon ... it held. This time.

She changed the wind, causing a brightly coloured bird to fly to the left instead of the right. The bird traveled past the window of a woman who was deciding on apprentices to hire. Cheered at its beauty, the woman decided to give the young girl the opportunity even though she had been a little clumsy in the earlier testing.

The Lady chose the way that sticks would float in a stream to delight some children, and the way that cards would fall to the floor after a dealer dropped a deck.

She also saw people praying to her. Praying for rain, or no rain, or the health of those who are ill, or for the day to happen in the way they wished. Thanking her in joy when they were lucky. Cursing her name when they were not.

A man named Francois asked that the toss of a coin would land one way, instead of the other. She ignored him, as she ignored all their calls for aid. There were no favourites under her cold gaze.

She moved over deserts, oceans, cities, and the dark spaces between stars ... and she gave everything its chance.

The Gambit cards can have two outcomes: success or failure. When this is applied to the Lady, the probability of each is precisely fifty-fifty. This card means that the situation is entirely up to chance and cannot be predicted.

This is of course not very helpful in most divination! The Court cards are large forces that affect us from outside. The Queen represents Lady Luck, and this card shows her in the purest form. But if chance is going to play such a large role, what can we do to get the best outcome? The obvious answer is to reduce the power of random chance to affect things.

This card is a warning that the situation can go anywhere, and unless that's exactly what we want then we need to reduce the danger through planning. Make lists and look at all the possible outcomes. Do what you can to prevent the worse ones. Only by working out all the possibilities can we decide which ones to secure ourselves against.

There is a positive view to this result as well. If this Gambit shows alongside another card that refers to a situation you thought was fixed, the introduction of pure chance means that better possibilities are out there than you thought. Fifty-fifty is a great result if you thought there was no hope or you are trying something that should be very difficult.

This Gambit suggests that a large amount of randomness or unpredictability affects events. It makes other cards unreliable—there's no bad intent from anyone or deliberate deceit, but the outcome is wild.

There is not much subtlety about this card, and no bargaining with it. Chance is a powerful and uncontrollable force.

QUEEN OF SPADES:
LADY'S FOLLY
"ELIN CLIMBS THE TOWER"

Bad Luck

In the Tower of Idrach is a turret room with circular white walls and a high ceiling. It is empty except for a large black sword that hangs suspended over a table by a thin chain.

The sword points downwards, and directly under the end of its sharp blade is a map of all the lands. As the heavy weapon swings back and forth, different towns and people come under its shadow.

Sometimes, the sword falls.

When the chain drops and the sword's deadly point pierces the map, bad luck is visited upon whichever life it points to. Terribly bad luck, a doom or curse.

Naturally, no one wants this fate to befall them. They hope and pray, and curse and weep.

One young woman named Elin decided to do more. She sought out the tower, climbed its walls, entered a window. She passed other rooms which held different instruments: a glass wand and a pink rose in a case in the first, jade spheres circling in the air in another, silver harps playing in a third.

She came to the room with the large black sword and took it off its chain, laying the metal weapon down onto the stone floor.

Then she left, thinking that she had saved her people.

But the next night, in the same room the sword was once again upon its chain, swinging back and forth across the map. Luck and chance must play their games in every home, and there must always be balance. In other parts of the Tower the treasures of life were bestowed: family, health, security, love. For them to be gifted to the people, the pendulum—and indeed the sword—must always return the other way.

There are negative cards in every divination deck. In this system (and frequently in playing card lore historically) the two most obvious are the Ace of Spades, and this one, the Queen of Spades. Its meaning is very simple: bad luck. There are no alternative or deeper definitions, that is all it says.

What can we do with this news? Not all luck can be good, and if a system is to include all possibilities, then it must also have cards with outcomes we don't want. It's what we *do* with that information that matters.

If you know that events could go badly, you can prepare. Even more than with the previous Lady's Gambit (where there is a high degree of randomness) suspecting that the luck will be bad in a situation gives you time to strengthen your defenses. It tells you not to rely on things turning out as they usually do, and to instead work at putting safety measures in place. Look at what you can control about the situation. Fix as much as you can so that luck will not affect it. Do the work now in case bad luck happens in the near future.

The Court cards are good at modifying other number cards. The combination with this one is not subtle: it's a big danger sign, and you need to stop what you're doing and prepare for it. Events cannot be relied on to take care of themselves or behave as normal. Assume the worst and do what you can to mitigate it.

Note that this is only about luck. It's not the same personal disaster as the Ace of Spades predicts, just an unfortunate turn of luck, and the outcome might not be very severe at all. It's a prompt to action instead of a decree of failure.

QUEEN OF HEARTS:
LADY'S TRIUMPH
"SAWYER AND THE FAERY"

Good Luck

Sawyer drank the magical potion. The liquid tasted of mint and dandelion root, because (although he didn't know this) that was all that it actually contained. The herbalist smiled at him and promised him a day of Good Luck.

He left the shop, and the herbalist changed into her true form and followed. She was a faery who had seen him walking along the path and decided that she loved him, and for that reason she was going to bring him summer days and joyful times.

He trod the forest track back to the village and did not know that two hungry wild dogs would have intercepted him—if they hadn't been distracted away by the faery's dancing lights.

Sawyer crossed a cornfield and found a lucky coin (which the faery had placed there moments before). He spent the coin on some bread and chewed it happily as he made his way to his house.

When he got there, he was just in time to see the edge of the roof above his door fall down—exactly where he would have been standing if he'd arrived a little sooner. By avoiding that injury, he was truly having a lucky day!

But the faery knew that it was not luck, for she took every action she could to preserve him and bring him happiness. It made her heart glow in return, and she vowed to reveal her true self to Sawyer one day soon.

What she did not know was that her Queen had seen the youth first and cast a genuine spell of luck upon him. It was this that brought his wanderings past the stream where the faery had been sitting, the only fairy who would love him instantly. Sawyer was right when he thought it—since the Queen had used a luck spell instead of direct intervention, all the later events of that day did indeed spring only from Good Luck. Not even faeries are immune to its power.

Lady's Triumph is a card that you always want to see. By delivering a large amount of good luck it makes every reading better, softening bad news and turning nice outcomes into really spectacular successes. In yes or no questions (or if you're evaluating the whole hand to see if it's positive or negative), this card is always a very big yes.

When this Triumph comes up as advice, it means that you can let luck and chance do some of the work for you. You still need to get to a place where luck can affect things, but once it's there you will be very fortunate. As with all the Court cards, this is an outside force instead of one from within you, so be sure to set up a situation that will let that outside force act as strongly as possible.

As the Triumph of the Lady cards, this one represents ultimate success for what she brings. Lady Luck is called on in every game of luck or chance, so her favour is always very powerful in a reading! Other aspects which come along with this include the emotions and results that good luck creates: happiness, safety, and positive outcomes.

This card signals that you can relax and let events carry on reliably with no bad surprises, because whenever something can go in the direction that is best for you, it will.

THE KINGS: THE SOVEREIGN

The Kings are the Role of the Sovereign. In every culture that has a ruler, regardless of gender, there is someone at the top of the ladder. In the European-style cards that have become playing cards, that is the King.

The Sovereign is the King of the castle—they set the rules, provide security and authority, and make decisions. Just like the Noble, this involves a contract with the people who depend on them. Where the Noble might be in charge of a home, family, or even just a few decisions that affect others, the Sovereign is a much larger power. The Role usually represents someone who has all the resources of a large institution backing them—a whole land instead of one household, with a focus on security and ruling.

We all come into contact with large institutions at some point, and their decisions can greatly affect us. When the King cards are drawn, we can tell that the issue comes from the whole of society or the influential forces within it.

KING OF CLUBS:
SOVEREIGN'S PROMISE
"XAVIER'S PRISON"

Security, Benevolent Institutions, Fulfilling Promises

Lord Xavier owned the old ruins on Falconer's Hill. There wasn't much left of them, some stone walls and good shelter from the outside if it got stormy or cold. In the centre of the main room was a trapdoor down to the dungeon, and that was a different place entirely. There the black stone sat thick and heavy on all sides. When you were inside the cell, the four walls felt as though they must be ten paces deep in every direction, only solid stone and the dependable earth beyond it. If you had been sentenced as a prisoner in his great-grandfather's time, you would not even have dreamed that you could escape. All around the quiet certainty of the stone spoke of timeless endurance.

Xavier was a good ruler; he cared for the people, and in return they allowed him to keep his place among them. He noticed what they needed and made it happen. One of the most unusual changes he made was to the lock of the prison in the ruins. He moved the lock to the inside of the cell instead of the outside.

The tradition of sanctuary started a few years ago, when a young man came from the south village. He would not speak but was clearly troubled and frightened. He walked among the ruins for a time and then climbed down into the prison.

When Xavier heard of this, he went to see the man. They talked a little and the visitor said that he was well but wished to be alone to think. Xavier let him do so. Eventually, the man came up from the dark dungeon and appeared rested, more sure of himself and more at peace. He thanked Xavier and walked over the hills to the east.

After that, other people started to visit the ruins for the same reason. There were usually two or three a year. Today it was a young woman in servant's clothes who said her name was Milly. She climbed down into the black, silent stone pit and closed the grate over her head, locking it with the bolt from the inside. Xavier asked her if anything was wrong, but she didn't want to talk about it, so he left her to the quiet she needed. He stayed upstairs and didn't push for answers or try to cheer her.

Milly sat surrounded by the heavy stone walls. Earlier that day, her body had felt as if it could be attacked from any direction and her mind had been full of whatever people could demand of her in the next instant. But the longer she stayed down there, the more her thoughts quietened. Nothing could possibly reach her through these walls. No one had asked her to do anything for hours now. And in the next few minutes, absolutely nothing would change. The dense rock had sat here for years and would continue exactly as it was.

Gradually, she felt herself becoming slower and stronger, to be like the giant blocks of stone. Eventually she unlocked the grate and raised it, climbed out, and thanked Lord Xavier for the use of his cell. Then she walked back to her home, looking happier and more confident.

His people thought that the gift Xavier gave was the use of his property, but he knew better. When questions would have been too much, he gave the visitors his silence until their own walls had returned.

The Sovereign sounds like a powerful being but—just like the Noble—they only exist in their high position because of a balance. A Sovereign's Promise is to the people they rule over, and the most fundamental part of that is to provide security to those people. The King of the castle has to share that castle in times of danger, or they won't keep it.

In the real world (unless you're close personal friends with a king) this card usually refers to a large institution, one which helps you. The Sovereign is compassionate and enthusiastic, aware of the physical needs of the people who rely on them but also in touch with their inner life and not chasing status for its own sake. Although the Court cards are not you, this security does become yours because providing it to others is exactly what the Sovereign does.

As well as benefitting from a powerful organisation, this card can be about whether you feel emotionally secure in any situation. The Sovereign's fortress can be one that you carry with you, your body feeling as though it's surrounded by a solid shell of rock, providing both physical safety and mental confidence.

When this card appears in readings, it can have some surprising effects. It often overrules and neutralizes any Trickster cards in the hand. It provides shelter from cards of conflict or bad luck. You have someone powerful on your side and their protection is impressive.

Rich people do not always keep their promises, so the fact that this one does means that the card also carries a meaning of deals being fulfilled honestly. The Promise cards are always linked to the ideal of a thing, the best version of it, and here the Sovereign keeps their word. This is a reading of people who have more power than you acting for good reasons, holding to their promises, and putting you in a secure and calm position.

KING OF DIAMONDS: SOVEREIGN'S GAMBIT
"MATTHEW AND THE BAKER"

Money, Diplomacy, Professional Services

Everyone knew that Baker Jones made the best pies. People came from all over just to buy them. Matthew Evans lived down the road but couldn't afford the baker's high prices; he would walk slowly past the shop with his brothers and sisters all sniffing the delicious fruit fillings of blackberries or cherry, or staring at a hot apple pie with a golden crust. Alas, these great treasures were held safely behind the window and stout wooden door, and none of his family had enough coin to actually buy a pie. Matthew had once tried to ask for cheaper prices but was quickly sent away with no doubt that such a thing would never happen.

This week was his younger sister's birthday, and they had planned to invite friends from the next town for a party. Naturally, the friends all asked if there would be any of the heavenly pies to eat. Matthew assured them (much to the surprise of his family) that there would.

When the day came, the party room was ... full of pies. Rhubarb, peach, hot jam fillings, strawberries, black currants, an open-topped prize-winner with cream and raspberries.

"However did you manage to buy these?" his sister asked with wide eyes.

"Well, old Jones wasn't going to lower his prices, so ... I humbly asked his daughter instead."

His older brother nudged him. "Nice work, you smooth talker! And she just said yes to all of this?"

"To this, and the part where I asked her to marry me."

And so there was a double celebration, to his sister's happiness and to the future of their family.

The Sovereign is a wealthy Role. King cards are typically very strong in games, and the one that symbolizes money as Diamonds is in control of a lot of riches.

A Sovereign achieves their goals using diplomacy, money, and the connections they have made. This is not the same as the loyalty of friends and family the Noble uses for a Gambit; instead it's a service from a professional person (or dealings with people much higher in society than us), particularly related to money and finance. The Sovereign has more than most people and spending it has always been part of diplomacy.

When we interact with a Sovereign it is usually someone big in the world or in a position of great authority over us. It could mean major assistance with financial matters or an indication that you should spend money now to gain the reward later. The Court cards are forces external to us so the person with the money is not necessarily you, but finance will influence the situation in some way.

On its own, this card primarily refers to money or the use of influence to make things happen. The outcome isn't known—although the Sovereign is powerful, the Gambit can still fail. The important part of this card is that money is moving. It is not an abundance of riches (something more represented by the King of Hearts) but a spinning coin, ready to fall one way or the other. The only reason one of the main definitions isn't "Gambling" is that the King represents large amounts of money, much more than would usually be gambled for fun. If this wealth is yours, be careful with it. If it isn't, someone is using influence in a way that will affect you.

KING OF SPADES:
SOVEREIGN'S FOLLY
"CALUM BREAKS THE OLD RULES"

Authority, Tradition, Inflexibility

Little Calum first showed his power in the village square, which was unfortunate. A bright arc of green light shot from his hand to the top of the tallest building and set it ablaze. The fire was dealt with easily, but everyone had seen what caused it and that meant trouble. It probably meant war.

The rules governing the wild magic had been written long ago and agreed upon by both kingdoms. No human was to possess the magic, and no aelf was to cross the border between their lands. In those days, magic was something that you could deliberately learn, and evil people tried to steal it for themselves. Outlawing it made sense. Those laws had held for as long as everyone could remember ... but now had been broken. It didn't matter that Calum was young and clearly didn't know how it had happened. The law was the law. He was sent to the palace.

King John was a wise ruler who had always kept a peace with the neighboring kingdom of Aelfland. When the news was brought to him, he was troubled. If the old law was not followed, the aelfs would demand to come across the border. The only way to avoid that (and a violent response from his own people) was to obey the ancient written rules: to kill the person who had used magic.

John went along with the boy to the edge of the forest on the border between the lands. There they waited. At dusk, when the shadows lengthened and then turned to grey and twilight, the Aelf King and his retinue appeared. John spoke first.

"The old laws have been broken, but not through any intent. This boy possesses the magic, without asking for it. The laws say that he must die but not one of my people thinks this would be justice. We seek another answer."

The Aelf King spoke in a friendly voice.

"If he is allowed to live, my people would want to come into your Kingdom. That would be a disaster. They are not ready and would forget themselves."

John swallowed nervously. "We do not want war."

The Aelf King thought for a moment, and then replied.

"Neither do we. I have decided. The boy can live." There were mutters of relief from both sides. "The old rules have kept us safe but they are not right in this situation. You say the boy did not seek power to harm others, he developed it naturally. He will be taught to control it so that none are harmed—on your side of the border or mine. As to our populations, I am in command of my people and I will tell them that we are not going to war. My authority will prevent it. Go in peace."

And he turned and left, merging with the shadows in the forest.

King John never knew what was said in the Aelf King's court, but the promise they had made held true: through the wisdom and leadership of both rulers, there was no war.

Tradition has its place, but in the hands of large institutions or authorities it rarely allows for a lot of individual freedom. The Folly of the very powerful Sovereign card is that they can come down on those beneath them with too much force and too little true understanding.

This is a card about being oppressed by authority. It could be due to a big organisation being too inflexible or an accepted idea in society too difficult to overcome. Either way, the result is a burden on everyone under it—and that may include the person the reading is for.

The previous two Sovereign cards brought friendly security and a focus on money. This one is much more of a warning, that someone in the world has more power than you and there is a chance they will apply it too rigidly. There are many groups and people that this Sovereign could describe: a parent, a business partner, a bank, a government, or all the people in a crowd in public. The only definition is that they have more authority than you.

Exactly what form the Folly takes varies quite widely. This is a card of people in power Getting It Wrong, or not being merciful. That could be the person affected by it facing financial problems or even suffering from the expectations of society against anyone in a minority group. Anything taboo or different could be met with resistance, anything requiring someone in power to help could face a blockage instead. The theme that links them all is that the action feels oppressive.

This is a problem which can still be solved, though. The other cards may show positive outcomes and the Sovereign is at least an outside force instead of one within you. That small detail can help! It means that the burden it brings to the situation is external and practical instead of internal or emotional.

The Sovereign is powerful, but so are you. Gather friends together and look at other routes for getting to your goal if bureaucracy or institutions block the way. If the reading suggests that you should act *like* this card, rely on traditional ways to bring a known route forwards to the situation. This is a strong power, and chaos will find it very difficult to overcome its slow and unimaginative rules.

KING OF HEARTS:
SOVEREIGN'S TRIUMPH
"VETTORIO'S CANVAS"

Help from a Master, Allies, Success in Traditional Ways

The studio was full of colourful paintings. Along every wall, on stands in every corner, and leaning up against chairs, the works of Master Domenico were all around. He was the most skilled artist in the land, rich and respected for his work. More than that, he was a good man—it was rare to see someone with his wealth who was so peaceful, compassionate, and still eager to learn new things even at his advanced age.

Young Vettorio was his apprentice but so far that had meant only that he was made to copy the Master's work precisely. When Domenico drew a building, Vettorio had to produce the same using identical brushstrokes. When Domenico went through a period of only using browns and dark greens, the student would be limited to those colours as well. The most usual subjects for their art were buildings in the city rendered with very straight lines and calm light.

Today was different. The old man sat down with the youth in the middle of all the painted canvases and opened a box that had previously been kept locked. Within it were paints and oils of the brightest colours!

"I have taught you the techniques I use and shown you the quality of art our patrons enjoy. Now, you must discover your own style."

Vettorio was overwhelmed. For months his brush had wanted to break free of the rigid lines and somber tones. Suddenly he felt a rush of affection for the older man he was apprenticed to. Some teachers remained strict and aloof, but the best became Mentors and used their influence to aid their students' progress.

The student hesitantly adjusted the blank canvas before him and reached for the new paints. Flaming crimson and buttercup yellow. Slowly, with nervous energy in his arm and a lightness in his heart, Vettorio drew the image worthy of those colours that first came to his mind, something unlike any other subject in this studio: the trailing, curving tailfeathers of a Firebird.

This is a wonderful card! It is extremely positive, in a secure and comfortable way. The Triumph of a Sovereign is to have it all: wealth, security, a strong castle, and the love of others. They spend their time enjoying physical abundance, food and drink, and a safe home. This Sovereign in particular is a mentor or patron, someone with more power than you who uses it to help you.

With the Aces counting as the number one in this deck, the King of Hearts is the top scoring card. Its message overpowers any other cards in the hand, overcomes any minor setbacks, and puts a positive spin on any flexible or ambiguous answers.

The King of Hearts has an interesting place in card history: it is known as the "Suicide King" and was thought to represent a French King stabbing himself with the sword. This is actually a myth—the design used to feature an axe instead, but bad copying by English printers made the axe's blade disappear. So while the King of Hearts was never meant to have a negative story, at least one unhappy legend grew up around it.

There's certainly none of that meaning here. This is the final card, signifying someone who is safe, rich and satisfied but who shows compassion and benevolence to others. They may demonstrate an attitude we should aspire to, or act as a friend we can lean on. This Sovereign is enjoying their rewards and everyone nearby benefits from that as well.

If this appears as an influence, we can welcome it. If it's an action which we should try to deliberately bring into our lives then we should seek help from a master, or one who has gained both security and happiness. Large institutions or powers can often feel remote or threatening, but when we find a way to benefit from them the rewards are substantial.

We should build our castle and aim to govern it as well (and as generously) as the best of those represented by this card.

SECTION THREE
EPILOGUE

I wanted to invent a divination system with tools that were cheap and easy for people to buy. My previous book had involved normal six-sided dice, so playing cards were an obvious choice as well. However, the magic of the cards very quickly took over the process.

Card games and their history are an enormous part of world culture and every country has their own: Japan's beautiful Hanafuda flower cards, the Egyptian and Middle-Eastern game of Basra, Vietnam's two-colour Chess cards, and Greenland's Voormsi, which uses 36 cards of the standard 52 deck. That's before we even get to the folklore and power of American Poker in the Old West or the modern casino.

Playing cards were never going to be a blank slate for me (or anyone) to write on; they have their own character which cannot be ignored. They bring a power to divination that can't be found anywhere else. This became obvious as soon as I started testing this system with friends, and they repeatedly asked for more readings "with that playing card deck you use." Of course it wasn't about the exact deck (a deliberately cheap mass-market plain deck of 52 cards with jokers) but the power of what the Clubs, Diamonds, Spades, and Hearts have come to mean to us all.

That said, there is no fixed system for playing card divination. A few such as Lenormand or Etteilla have been recorded historically but very few readers end up using the definitions precisely as written when performing kitchen table fortune-telling. Nearly everyone modifies their own (and each of the modern books in the Bibliography section say this too). So it has been an honor to ride the power of the cards while also adding new stories to them. I hope that many people will pick up their own decks and find great experiences in the shuffle.

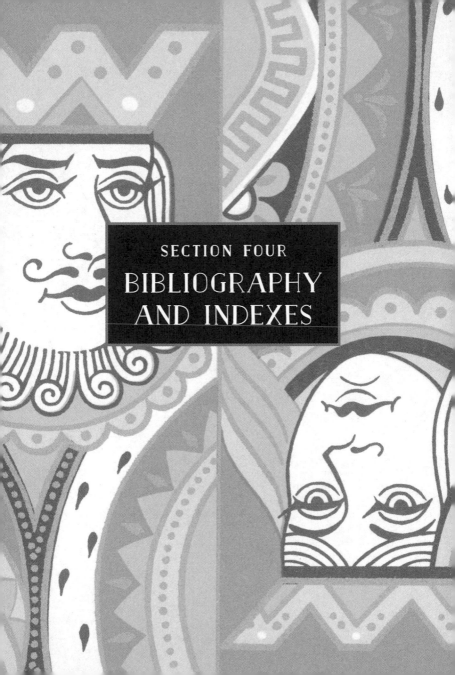

SECTION FOUR

BIBLIOGRAPHY AND INDEXES

BIBLIOGRAPHY

Benham, W. Gurney. *Playing cards: History of the pack and explanations of its many secrets*. London: Spring Books, 1931.

Dee, Jonathan. *Fortune Telling Using Playing Cards*. Charlottesville, VA: Hampton Roads Publishing Co, 2004.

Field, Albert. *Transformation Playing Cards*. Stamford, CT: U.S. Games Systems, 1987.

Hargrave, Catherine Perry. *A History of Playing Cards*. New York: Houghton Mifflin company, 1930.

Hutcheson, Cory Thomas. *54 Devils: The Art and Folklore of Fortune-Telling with Playing Cards*. [n.l.]: Createspace, 2013.

St. Lawrence, Chita. *It's All in the Cards*. New York: Perigee, 1999.

Taylor, Rev. Ed. S. *The Story of Playing Cards: Anecdotes for Their Use in Conjuring, Fortune Telling and Card Sharping*. London: John Camden Hotten, 1865.

Various. *Dr. Flamstead's and Mr. Patridge's new fortune-book*. London, 1729.

Webster, Richard. *Playing Card Divination for Beginners: Fortune Telling with Ordinary Cards*. St. Paul, MN: Llewellyn Publications, 2002.

INDEX OF CARDS
BY NUMBER

INDEX OF
CARDS BY SUIT

To Write to the Author

If you wish to contact the author or would like more information about this book, please write to the author in care of Llewellyn Worldwide Ltd. and we will forward your request. Both the author and publisher appreciate hearing from you and learning of your enjoyment of this book and how it has helped you. Llewellyn Worldwide Ltd. cannot guarantee that every letter written to the author can be answered, but all will be forwarded. Please write to:

Stephen Ball
℅ Llewellyn Worldwide
2143 Wooddale Drive
Woodbury, MN 55125-2989

Please enclose a self-addressed stamped envelope for reply,
or $1.00 to cover costs. If outside the U.S.A., enclose
an international postal reply coupon.

Many of Llewellyn's authors have websites with additional information and resources. For more information, please visit our website at http://www.llewellyn.com.